Best of
ETHIOPIAN
Comforts made simple

GARDEN
of **GRAPES.**

Second Edition: 2024

Published by Garden of Grapes.

Printed in USA

The recipes, techniques, and tips in this cookbook are intended for personal use only. The author and publisher are not responsible for any adverse effects or consequences resulting from the use of the recipes or suggestions in this book.

Library of Congress Cataloging-in-Publication Data:

Second edition.

Manufactured in USA
www.gardenofgrapes.com

Introduction

Ladies and gentlemen, fellow culinary adventurers,

Welcome to the vibrant world of the "Ethiopian Comforts Cookbook: Flavors of Ethiopia - 100+ Authentic Home Comforts Made Easy for Home Cook." As you turn these pages and embark on a journey through the rich and diverse flavors of Ethiopia, I extend to you a warm and heartfelt welcome.

This cookbook is a celebration of the soul-soothing and heartwarming dishes that have graced Ethiopian homes for generations. It is a testament to the comfort that comes from a shared meal, the warmth of a welcoming kitchen, and the vibrant tapestry of flavors that make up Ethiopian cuisine.

The inspiration behind this cookbook was born from a deep appreciation for the incredible diversity of Ethiopian culinary traditions. Ethiopia, often called the "Land of Thirteen Months of Sunshine," is a place where ancient cooking techniques, bold spices, and a deep respect for nature come together to create a cuisine like no other. It's a cuisine that has captured my heart, and I hope it captures yours too.

Within the pages of this cookbook, you'll find a treasure trove of recipes that span the length and breadth of Ethiopia. From the fiery stews of the Amhara region to the delicate injera bread that's a staple in every Ethiopian meal, we've taken the intricate and made it accessible. Whether you're a seasoned home cook or just beginning your culinary journey, you'll find dishes that will transport you to the heart of Ethiopia without leaving your own kitchen.

But this cookbook is not just a collection of recipes. It's an invitation to explore a rich culinary culture, to embrace the joys of cooking and sharing meals with loved ones, and to embark on a journey that transcends borders and cultures. It's a testament to the power of food to bring people together, to comfort the soul, and to celebrate the diversity of our world.

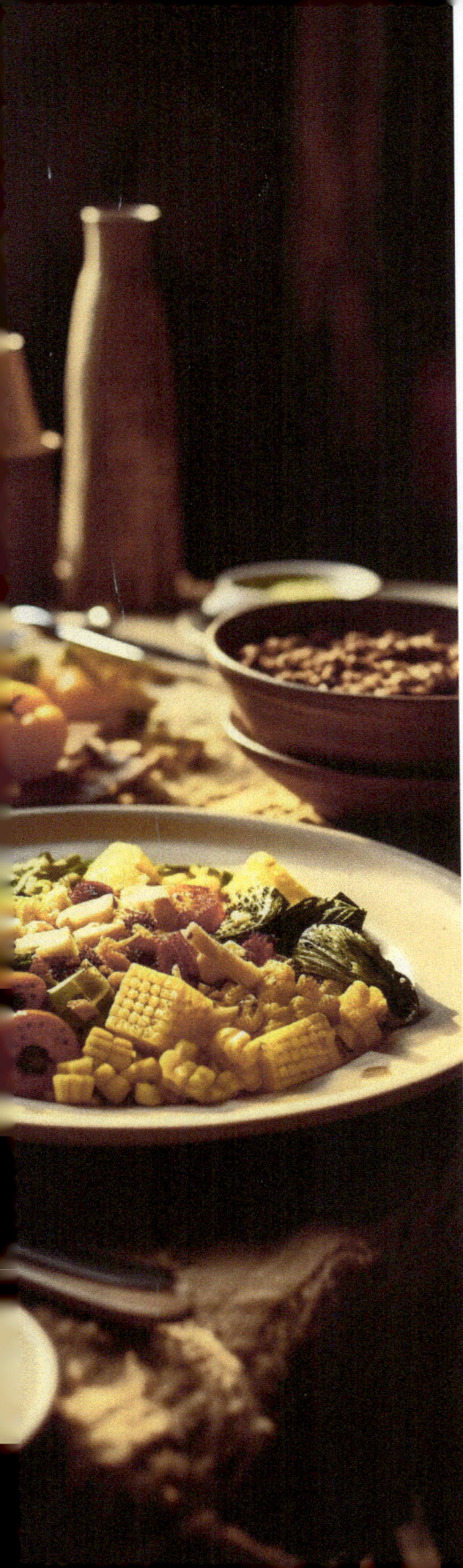

So, as you flip through these pages, I encourage you to immerse yourself in the flavors of Ethiopia. Try your hand at making injera from scratch, savor the aroma of berbere spices, and relish the hearty doro wat simmering on your stove. And as you do, remember that you're not just cooking a meal—you're creating an experience, a connection, and a piece of culinary history.

Thank you for joining me on this culinary adventure. I hope this cookbook brings you the same comfort, joy, and sense of discovery that Ethiopian cuisine has brought to my life. Enjoy the journey, and may your kitchen be filled with the enticing aromas and delicious flavors of Ethiopia. Bon appétit!

Sambusas (Ethiopian Samosas)
See page, 14

Cooking Philosophy or Approach

Lovers of Ethiopian cuisine, home cooks, and culinary adventurers,

Welcome to the heart and soul of Ethiopian Comforts, where we embark on a journey through the vibrant and rich flavors of Ethiopia. In this cookbook, I want to share with you not just recipes, but a culinary philosophy—a way of approaching food that celebrates tradition, simplicity, and the joy of sharing a meal.

Ethiopian cuisine is a treasure trove of bold spices, hearty stews, and communal dining. It's a cuisine that thrives on the art of simplicity, where a handful of ingredients can transform into a symphony of flavors that dance on your taste buds. It's a cuisine that values time-honored techniques, where slow-cooking and the art of balance create dishes that are both comforting and exhilarating.

At the heart of this cookbook is my deep respect for the culinary traditions of Ethiopia. You'll find recipes that honor the classics, from injera to doro wat, and introduce you to lesser-known gems from different regions of this diverse country. You'll discover the magic of berbere spice, the earthiness of lentils, and the comforting embrace of aromatic stews.

The key to Ethiopian cooking lies in the balance of flavors—the spicy, the savory, the sour, and the sweet. It's a balance that has been perfected over generations, and I encourage you to embrace it, experiment with it, and make it your own.

When it comes to ingredients, we stay true to the authenticity of Ethiopian cuisine while making it accessible for the home cook. You'll find a guide to sourcing and using traditional ingredients, and where necessary, suitable substitutes that ensure you can create these flavors in your own kitchen.

As for technique, the heart of Ethiopian cooking is the slow simmer—the patient coaxing of flavors and textures from simple ingredients. It's the art of building layers of taste over time, allowing the alchemy of spices to weave their magic. You'll find step-by-step instructions that guide you through these techniques, ensuring that your home-cooked Ethiopian meals are nothing short of spectacular.

In essence, this cookbook is an invitation to explore Ethiopia through its food, to savor the comforts of this remarkable cuisine, and to share the joy of a communal meal. It's about embracing a culinary journey that's steeped in tradition but open to interpretation, where every meal is a celebration of culture and community.

So, as you dive into the recipes within these pages, remember that Ethiopian Comforts is not just about cooking. It's about connecting—with the flavors, the traditions, and the people you share your meal with. May your kitchen be filled with the enticing aromas of Ethiopian spices, and may your table be a place of warmth and togetherness.

Enjoy the journey, and may your love for Ethiopian cuisine grow with each dish you create.

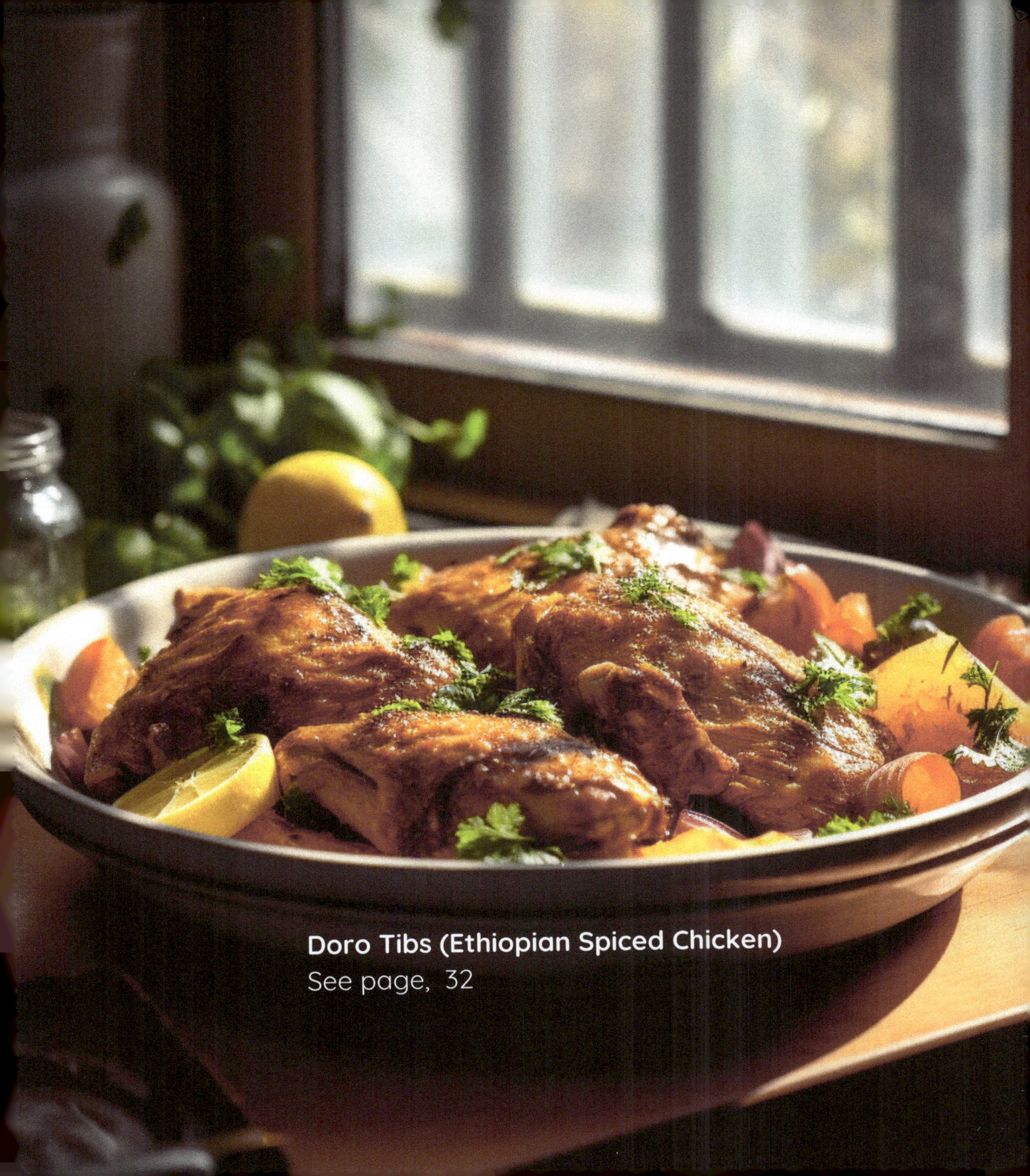

Doro Tibs (Ethiopian Spiced Chicken)
See page, 32

Tips for Successful Cooking

My friends, as we delve into the rich and aromatic world of Ethiopian cuisine within the pages of the "Ethiopian Comforts Cookbook: Flavors of Ethiopia - 100+ Authentic Home Comforts Made Easy," I'd like to share some essential tips and guidance to ensure your culinary journey is a resounding success.

1. Spice Selection: Ethiopian cuisine is celebrated for its bold and flavorful spices. When selecting spices for your dishes, opt for high-quality, fresh spices whenever possible. Toast whole spices before grinding to release their full fragrance and flavor.

2. Berbere Spice Blend: Berbere is the heart and soul of Ethiopian cooking. It's a fiery blend of chili peppers, herbs, and spices. You can make it from scratch or find it in stores, but always adjust the amount to suit your heat tolerance.

3. Injera Preparation: Injera, the spongy sourdough flatbread, is a staple in Ethiopian meals. Preparing injera can be a bit tricky, but practice makes perfect. Ensure your batter is well-fermented for that characteristic tangy flavor. Use a non-stick skillet or injera pan for the best results.

4. Slow Cooking: Many Ethiopian dishes benefit from slow and patient cooking. Low, gentle simmering allows flavors to meld, creating that signature depth. Don't rush the process; let the aromas fill your kitchen.

5. Lentils and Legumes: Lentils and legumes are a key source of protein in Ethiopian cuisine. Be sure to rinse and sort them before cooking to remove any debris. Red lentils are a popular choice due to their quick cooking time.

6. Wat or Stew: Wat, the savory and aromatic stew, is a cornerstone of Ethiopian meals. Cook wats slowly and be prepared to spend time building layers of flavor. The result is well worth the effort.

7. Teff Flour: Teff, the tiny grain used to make injera, can be challenging to find in some regions. Look for specialty stores or online sources for teff flour. Remember to allow the batter to ferment, as this is crucial for the unique taste of injera.

8. Fresh Herbs: Ethiopian cuisine also features fresh herbs like cilantro and parsley, which add a vibrant touch to many dishes. Use them generously for that authentic flavor.

9. Enjoy the Process: Ethiopian cooking is an experience to savor. Embrace the slow, methodical approach, and don't be afraid to get your hands dirty. The tactile nature of rolling injera and savoring the communal aspect of Ethiopian dining is a big part of the joy.

Remember, dear readers, Ethiopian cuisine is a journey of flavors and traditions. Don't be discouraged if your first attempt isn't perfect. With each dish, you'll refine your techniques and uncover the nuances of this captivating culinary tradition. So, gather your ingredients, invite your loved ones to the table, and embark on a flavorful adventure through Ethiopia's rich and diverse comfort foods. Happy cooking!

Kitchen Essentials

Welcome to the vibrant world of Ethiopian cuisine, where flavors are bold, spices are aromatic, and communal dining is a cherished tradition. As we dive into the "Ethiopian Comforts Cookbook: Flavors of Ethiopia - 100+ Authentic Home Comforts Made Easy for Home Cook," let's make sure you're well-equipped to embark on this culinary adventure.

Kitchen Essentials:

1. Injera Griddle (Mitad): The heart of Ethiopian cooking, this round, flat griddle is essential for making injera, the spongy and tangy Ethiopian bread. You can also use a large non-stick skillet as a substitute.

2. Berbere Spice: This fiery and complex spice blend is a cornerstone of Ethiopian cuisine. It typically includes chili peppers, garlic, ginger, fenugreek, and other aromatic spices. You can buy it pre-made or make your own for an authentic touch.

3. Njera (Injera): This unique sourdough flatbread is a staple in Ethiopian meals. While it's traditionally made at home, you can also find it in specialty stores or opt for a mix to make your own.

4. Teff Flour: The tiny grain used to make injera. It's gluten-free and packed with nutrients. You'll need this for injera preparation.

5. Mesob: A traditional Ethiopian table, often woven from straw. While not a must, it adds an authentic touch to your dining experience.

6. Coffee Pot (Jebena): If you want to savor the Ethiopian coffee ceremony, you'll need a jebena, a uniquely designed coffee pot.

7. Spice Grinder: To freshly grind spices like cardamom, cloves, and cinnamon for various dishes.

8. Large Pot: For preparing stews like Doro Wat or Misir Wat. A Dutch oven works perfectly.

9. Knife and Cutting Board: Standard tools for chopping vegetables and meat.

Tips on How to Use These Tools Effectively:

1. Injera Making: Injera batter is fermented, so allow it to rest for at least 24 hours before cooking. Use a non-stick griddle or skillet and swirl the batter quickly to create the characteristic spongy texture.

2. Berbere Spice: Experiment with the level of heat you prefer. It's the backbone of many Ethiopian dishes, so find the right balance for your taste.

3. Njera (Injera): When cooking injera, start with a medium-hot griddle and cover it with a lid to create steam, ensuring even cooking.

4. Teff Flour: Store it in an airtight container to keep it fresh and free from moisture.

5. Coffee Ceremony: If you're indulging in the Ethiopian coffee tradition, use freshly roasted beans for the best flavor. Roast them over low heat and serve with popcorn for a delightful pairing.

6. Spice Grinder: Grind spices in small batches to maintain freshness, and clean it thoroughly between different spices to avoid flavor contamination.

With these kitchen essentials and tips in hand, you're ready to embark on your Ethiopian culinary journey. Whether you're preparing classic dishes like Doro Wat or exploring lesser-known gems, may your kitchen be filled with the irresistible aromas of Ethiopia, and your table with the warmth of shared meals and culture. Enjoy!

Taita (Ethiopian Porridge)
See page, 62

Flavor Pairing Suggestions

Ladies and gentlemen, fellow culinary adventurers,

As we venture further into the vibrant tapestry of Ethiopian cuisine within the "Ethiopian Comforts Cookbook: Flavors of Ethiopia - 100+ Authentic Home Comforts Made Easy for Home Cook," I want to take a moment to dive into the heart of flavor pairings. It's in these combinations of tastes, textures, and ingredients that the magic of Ethiopian cooking truly comes alive.

In the world of Ethiopian cuisine, flavors dance and intertwine, creating a symphony of tastes that awaken the senses. Here, it's not just about what ingredients you use but how they play together to create something greater than the sum of their parts. So, let's explore some flavor pairing suggestions that can help you experiment, innovate, and craft your own Ethiopian-inspired culinary creations.

1. Berbere Spice and Sweetness: The fiery warmth of berbere spice, a cornerstone of Ethiopian cooking, pairs wonderfully with a touch of sweetness. Consider incorporating honey, dried fruits like apricots, or caramelized onions into your dishes for a beautiful balance of flavors.

2. Injera and Stews: Injera, the spongy and slightly tangy Ethiopian flatbread, is the perfect foil for hearty stews. The injera's sour notes complement the rich, savory stews, creating a harmonious bite. Tear off a piece of injera, scoop up your stew, and savor the fusion of textures and tastes.

3. Garlic and Ginger: The dynamic duo of Ethiopian cuisine, garlic, and ginger, add depth and complexity to many dishes. Whether you're sautéing vegetables or marinating proteins, this combination brings layers of flavor that are both aromatic and earthy.

4. Lentils and Spices: Ethiopian lentil dishes, such as Misir Wat, are a vegetarian delight. Pair the nutty richness of lentils with a blend of spices like cumin, coriander, and paprika for a flavor explosion that's both hearty and satisfying.

5. Teff and Creaminess: Teff, the smallest grain in the world and the basis for injera, has a nutty flavor that pairs wonderfully with creamy elements. Think about incorporating coconut milk, yogurt, or tahini into your teff-based recipes to create a luxurious contrast.

6. Raw and Cooked: Ethiopian cuisine often embraces contrasts. Consider adding a refreshing salad of tomatoes, cucumbers, and herbs as a side to a warm, spicy stew. The cool, crisp textures balance the heat and richness of the main dish.

7. Citrus and Heat: Ethiopian cuisine isn't shy about spices, and citrus provides a delightful counterpoint. A squeeze of lemon or lime juice can brighten up your dishes, cut through richness, and add a zesty dimension to your meals.

Remember, Ethiopian cooking is an art, and these pairings are merely a starting point. Embrace your inner chef, experiment with different combinations, and let your taste buds be your guide. Whether you're following a traditional recipe or creating your own culinary masterpiece, the flavors of Ethiopia are yours to explore, savor, and share with the world.

So, go forth, fellow cooks, and may your Ethiopian-inspired creations be a celebration of flavors, a testament to your culinary curiosity, and a source of joy at your table. Enjoy the journey, for it's in the art of pairing flavors that we discover the true essence of a cuisine. Happy cooking!

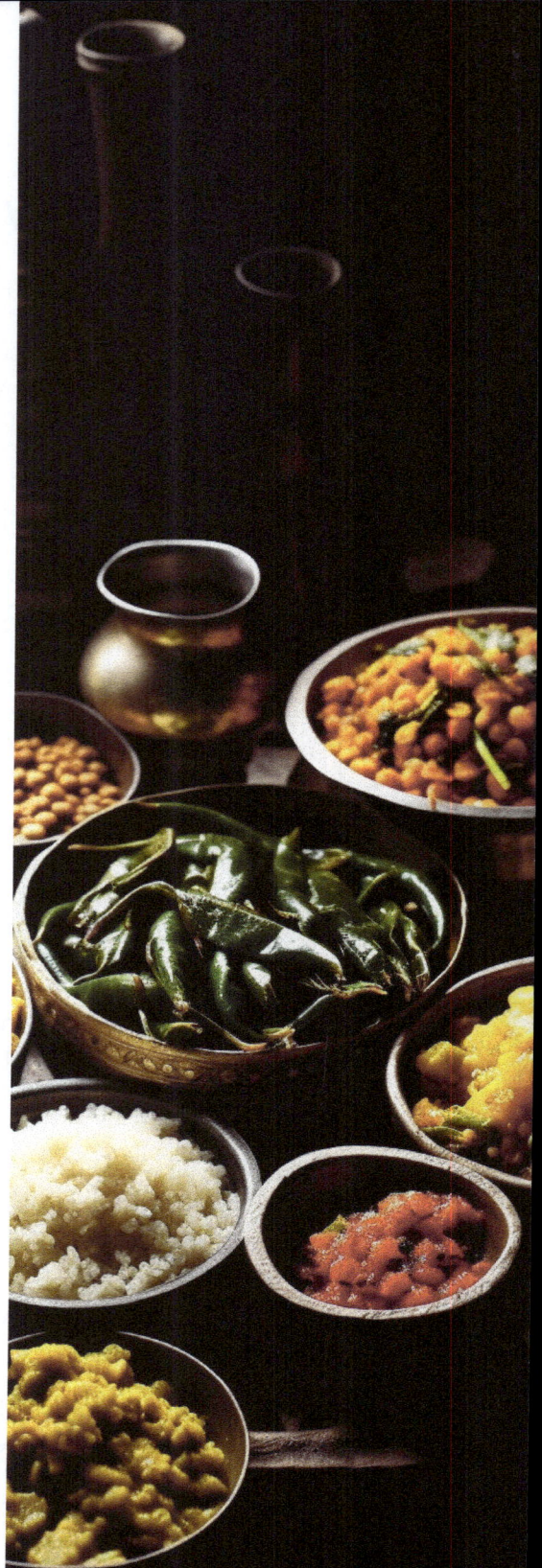

Table of contents

Chapter 1:
Breakfast

Doro Wat and Injera

mmmmmmmmmmm

Ingredients:

- 4 chicken drumsticks
- 2 onions
- 4 cloves garlic
- 2 tbsp berbere spice
- 2 tbsp vegetable oil
- 1 cup chicken broth
- Salt & pepper to taste
- Injera (store-bought or homemade)

2   **kcal 450**   **90**

Normal

A taste of Ethiopia: Doro Wat, a spicy chicken stew, and injera, a spongy sourdough flatbread, make a hearty breakfast duo.

Directions

1. Marinate chicken in berbere spice, garlic, and salt for 30 min.
2. Sauté onions until golden, add chicken and cook until browned.
3. Add broth, simmer for 45 min.
4. Serve hot with injera.
5. Tear injera, scoop doro wat, and enjoy!

Ful Medames

〰〰〰〰〰〰〰〰

Ingredients:

- 1 cup dried fava beans
- 2 cloves garlic
- 2 tbsp olive oil
- 1 tsp cumin
- Salt & pepper to taste
- Lemon wedges

Ful Medames: Creamy fava bean stew, a beloved Ethiopian breakfast.

Directions

1. Soak beans overnight, then boil until tender.
2. Sauté garlic in olive oil, add cooked beans.
3. Mash slightly, add cumin, salt, and pepper.
4. Serve with lemon wedges.

Substitutions

- Canned fava beans

| 2 | 320 | 20 |

Chechebsa

Ingredients:

- 2 cups all-purpose flour
- 2 tsp berbere spice
- 2 tbsp vegetable oil
- Salt to taste
- Honey (optional)
- Nigella seeds (optional)

Chechebsa: Crispy, spiced flatbread cubes with a kick of heat.

Directions

1. Mix flour, berbere spice, and salt, add water to form a dough.
2. Roll out, cut into squares, and deep-fry until crispy.
3. Drizzle with honey and sprinkle nigella seeds if desired.
4. Serve hot.

1   **280**   **25**

Genfo

Ingredients:

- 1/2 cup barley flour
- 1/4 cup teff flour
- 1/4 cup butter
- 2 tbsp berbere spice
- Honey to taste
- Milk (optional)

Genfo: A warm Ethiopian porridge to start your day with comfort.

Directions

1. Mix barley and teff flours, add butter, and berbere spice.
2. Cook on low, stirring until it forms a dough-like consistency.
3. Serve with honey and a splash of milk if desired.

Substitutions

- Use wheat flour instead

Kita: Thin, crispy Ethiopian flatbread perfect for dipping.

1   180   30

Kita

Ingredients:

- 1 cup all-purpose flour
- 1/2 cup water
- 2 tbsp vegetable oil
- Salt to taste

Directions

1. Mix flour, water, and salt to form a smooth dough.
2. Divide into small balls, roll out thin.
3. Cook in a hot, oiled pan until golden on both sides.
4. Serve warm.

1   **220**   **45**

Ambasha

Ingredients:

- 3 cups all-purpose flour
- 1/2 cup sugar
- 1/2 cup milk
- 1/4 cup butter
- 2 tsp yeast
- 1/2 tsp cardamom
- 1/4 tsp nutmeg

Substitutions

- Use margarine instead

Normal

Ambasha: Sweet, fragrant Ethiopian bread, a delightful treat.

Directions

1. Mix flour, sugar, yeast, cardamom, and nutmeg.
2. Add milk and knead into a soft dough.
3. Let it rise for 2 hours.
4. Shape into a round loaf, bake at 350°F for 30 min.
5. Enjoy the sweet aroma!

2   **280**   **15**

Ethiopian Scrambled Eggs

Ingredients:

- 4 eggs
- 1/2 onion
- 1 tomato
- 2 tbsp butter
- Salt & pepper to taste

Scrambled eggs, Ethiopian style: a quick and tasty breakfast.

Directions

1. Sauté onions in butter until translucent.
2. Add tomatoes, cook until soft.
3. Beat eggs, pour over veggies, scramble until set.
4. Season with salt and pepper, serve hot.

Atakilt Wat

Ingredients:

- 1/2 cabbage
- 2 carrots
- 1 potato
- 1 onion
- 2 cloves garlic
- 2 tbsp vegetable oil
- 1 tsp turmeric
- Salt & pepper to taste

Easy

2 | 210 | 30

Atakilt Wat: Ethiopian cabbage dish, a flavorful morning choice.

Directions

1. Sauté onions, garlic, and turmeric in oil.
2. Add chopped veggies, cook until tender.
3. Season with salt and pepper.
4. Serve hot.

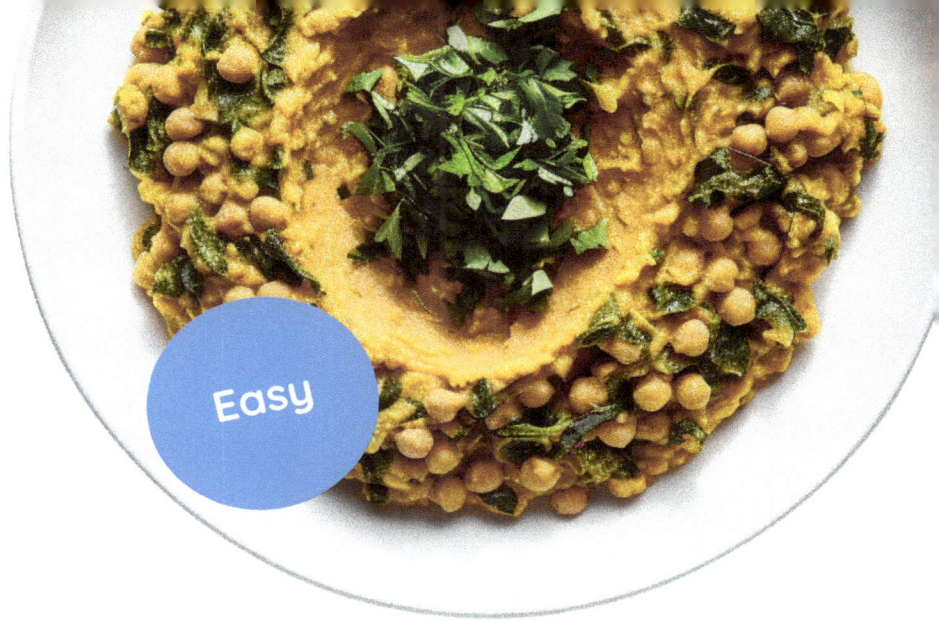

2   160   10

Buticha

~~~~~~~~~~

Ingredients:

- 1 cup chickpea flour
- 1/4 cup olive oil
- 1/2 onion
- 2 cloves garlic
- 1 tsp berbere spice
- Salt to taste

Easy

Buticha: Creamy Ethiopian chickpea dip, perfect for breakfast.

Directions

1. Sauté onions and garlic in olive oil until fragrant.
2. Add chickpea flour and berbere spice, cook until golden.
3. Add water to make a smooth dip.
4. Season with salt and serve with bread.

2 **240** **25**

Ingudai Tibs

~~munmunmunmun~~

Ingredients:

- 2 cups mushrooms
- 1 onion
- 2 cloves garlic
- 2 tbsp olive oil
- 1 tsp paprika
- Salt & pepper to taste

Easy

Ingudai Tibs: Sautéed mushrooms with spices, an Ethiopian delight.

Directions

1. Sauté onions and garlic in olive oil until soft.
2. Add mushrooms, cook until browned.
3. Season with paprika, salt, and pepper.
4. Serve hot with injera.

Substitutions

- Use other mushrooms

Chapter 2:
Appetizers and Snacks

2 **320** **20**

Injera with Dips (Tikil Gomen and Shiro)

Ingredients:

- Injera (store-bought or homemade)
- For Tikil Gomen:
 - 1/2 cabbage
 - 1 carrot
 - 1 onion
 - 2 cloves garlic
 - 2 tbsp vegetable oil
 - 1 tsp turmeric
- For Shiro:
 - 1 cup Shiro powder
 - 2 cups water
 - 2 tbsp vegetable oil
 - 2 cloves garlic
 - Salt to taste

Normal

Injera, the star, served with Tikil Gomen (cabbage) and Shiro (chickpea) dips.

Directions

1. Prepare injera or warm store-bought injera.
2. For Tikil Gomen:
 a. Sauté onions, garlic, and turmeric in oil.
 b. Add chopped cabbage and carrot, cook until tender.
 c. Season with salt.
3. For Shiro:
 a. Mix Shiro powder with water.
 b. Sauté garlic in oil, add the Shiro mixture, and simmer until it thickens.
 c. Add salt to taste.
4. Serve injera with dips.

2 260 45

Sambusas (Ethiopian Samosas)

Ingredients:

- 10 spring roll wrappers
- 1/2 lb ground beef or lentils
- 1 onion
- 2 cloves garlic
- 1 tsp berbere spice
- 2 tbsp vegetable oil
- Salt & pepper to taste

Sambusas: Crispy pastry filled with spiced meat or lentils, an Ethiopian favorite.

Directions

1. For the filling:
 a. Sauté onions and garlic in oil until soft.
 b. Add ground beef or lentils, cook until browned.
 c. Season with berbere spice, salt, and pepper.
2. Fill spring roll wrappers, fold into triangles, and seal edges with water.
3. Deep-fry until golden.
4. Serve hot.

Substitutions

- Use phyllo dough

1 | 420 | 15

Kitfo (Ethiopian Steak Tartare)

Ingredients:

- 1/2 lb ground beef
- 1 tsp mitmita spice
- 1 tsp cardamom
- 2 tbsp niter kibbeh (spiced clarified butter)
- Injera or bread for serving
- Salt to taste

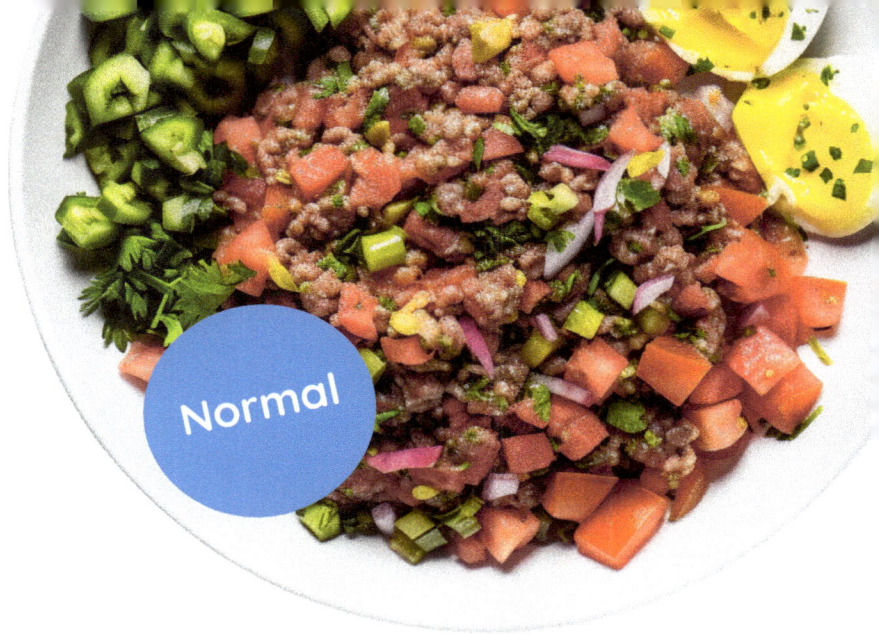

Normal

Kitfo: Raw minced beef, seasoned with spices, a bold and traditional snack.

Directions

1. Mix ground beef with mitmita spice and cardamom.
2. Sauté the beef in niter kibbeh until browned.
3. Season with salt.
4. Serve with injera or bread.

2 | 180 | 30

Azifa (Ethiopian Lentil Salad)

Ingredients:

- 1 cup green lentils
- 1/2 onion
- 2 cloves garlic
- 2 tbsp olive oil
- 2 tsp mustard
- 1 tsp vinegar
- Salt & pepper to taste

Easy

Azifa: Tangy lentil salad with a burst of flavors, perfect for snacking.

Directions

1. Boil lentils until tender, then drain.
2. Sauté onions and garlic in olive oil until soft.
3. Mix mustard, vinegar, salt, and pepper.
4. Toss lentils in the dressing, serve chilled.

2 | **220** | **10**

Quanta Firfir (Ethiopian Beef Jerky)

Ingredients:

- 1/2 lb Quanta (Ethiopian beef jerky)
- 2 cups injera crumbs
- 2 tbsp vegetable oil
- 2 tsp berbere spice
- Salt & pepper to taste

Normal

Quanta Firfir: Spicy Ethiopian beef jerky sautéed with injera crumbs.

Directions

1. Soak Quanta in hot water until soft, then cut into strips.
2. Sauté Quanta in vegetable oil until slightly crispy.
3. Add injera crumbs and berbere spice, sauté until well mixed.
4. Season with salt and pepper.
5. Serve warm.

Substitutions

- Use beef jerky

Dulet (Ethiopian Organ Meat Stew)

Ingredients:

- 1/2 lb mixed organ meats (liver, kidney, and tripe)
- 1 onion
- 2 cloves garlic
- 2 tbsp niter kibbeh (spiced clarified butter)
- 1 tsp berbere spice
- Salt & pepper to taste

Dulet: A spicy Ethiopian stew made with organ meats, not for the faint-hearted.

Directions

1. Clean and chop organ meats into small pieces.
2. Sauté onions and garlic in niter kibbeh until soft.
3. Add organ meats, berbere spice, salt, and pepper.
4. Cook until the meats are tender.
5. Serve hot.

Substitutions

- Use only liver

2 · 320 · 30 · Hard

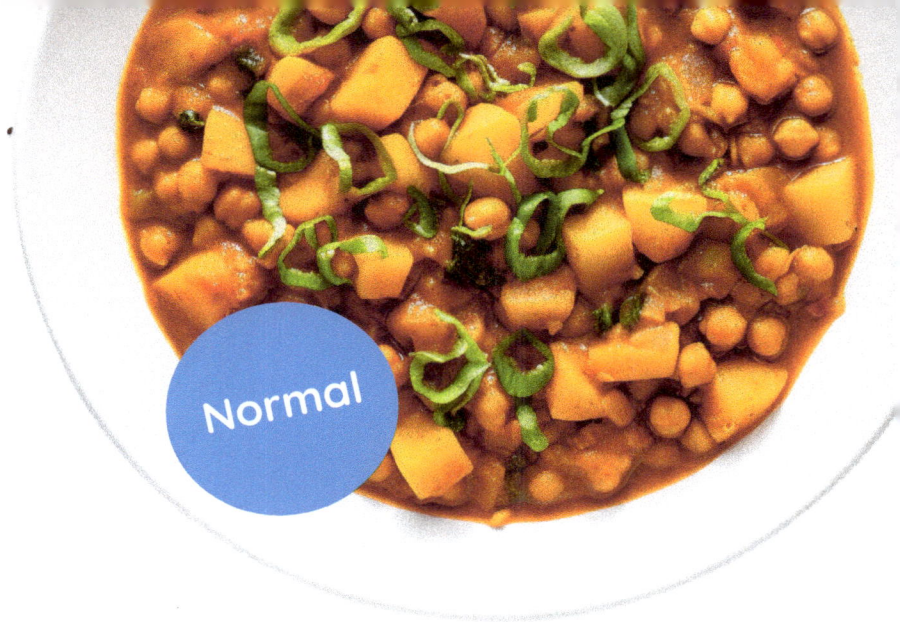

2   **250**   **25**

Shiro (Ethiopian Chickpea Stew)

Ingredients:

- 1 cup Shiro powder
- 2 cups water
- 2 tbsp vegetable oil
- 2 cloves garlic
- Salt to taste

Normal

Shiro: A rich, flavorful chickpea stew, perfect for dipping injera.

Directions

1. Mix Shiro powder with water.
2. Sauté garlic in vegetable oil until fragrant.
3. Add the Shiro mixture and simmer until thickened.
4. Season with salt.
5. Serve hot for dipping.

2 | 220 | 20

Fitfit (Ethiopian Bread Salad)

Ingredients:

- 2 cups torn injera
- 2 tomatoes
- 1/2 cucumber
- 1/4 onion
- 2 cloves garlic
- 2 tbsp olive oil
- 1 tsp berbere spice
- Salt & pepper to taste

Fitfit: A refreshing Ethiopian salad with torn injera, veggies, and a zesty dressing.

Directions

1. Soak torn injera briefly in water, then squeeze out excess.
2. Dice tomatoes, cucumber, and onions.
3. Sauté garlic in olive oil until fragrant.
4. Add berbere spice, salt, and pepper.
5. Toss everything together and serve.

2 | **160** | **30**

Dabo Kolo (Ethiopian Spiced Snack)

Ingredients:

- 2 cups all-purpose flour
- 2 tsp berbere spice
- 1/4 cup vegetable oil
- 1/4 cup water
- Salt to taste
- Oil for frying

Easy

Dabo Kolo: Crunchy, spiced Ethiopian snacks, perfect for munching.

Directions

1. Mix flour, berbere spice, and salt.
2. Add vegetable oil and water to form a dough.
3. Roll into small balls, flatten, and cut into shapes.
4. Deep-fry until golden.
5. Let cool before munching.

Substitutions

- Use chili powder

2 **140** **40**

Kolo (Roasted Barley Snack)

Ingredients:

- 1 cup roasted barley
- 1/4 cup peanuts
- 1/4 cup chickpeas
- 1/4 cup sunflower seeds
- 1/4 cup pumpkin seeds
- Salt to taste

Kolo: Nutty roasted barley snack, a popular street food in Ethiopia.

Directions

1. Mix all ingredients together.
2. Season with salt to taste.
3. Store in an airtight container for a crunchy snack.

Chapter 3:
Soups and Stews

2 450 90

Doro Wat (Ethiopian Chicken Stew)

Normal

Doro Wat: A rich and spicy Ethiopian chicken stew, a culinary masterpiece.

Ingredients:

- 4 chicken drumsticks
- 2 onions
- 4 cloves garlic
- 2 tbsp berbere spice
- 2 tbsp vegetable oil
- 1 cup chicken broth
- Salt & pepper to taste

Directions

1. Marinate chicken in berbere spice, garlic, and salt for 30 min.
2. Sauté onions until golden, add chicken and cook until browned.
3. Add broth, simmer for 45 min.
4. Serve hot with injera.
5. Tear injera, scoop doro wat, and enjoy!

2   **380**   **75**

Tibs Wat (Ethiopian Beef Stew)

Tibs Wat: A hearty Ethiopian beef stew with a spicy kick, a true comfort food.

Ingredients:

- 1/2 lb beef (cubed)
- 2 onions
- 4 cloves garlic
- 2 tbsp berbere spice
- 2 tbsp niter kibbeh (spiced clarified butter)
- Salt & pepper to taste

Directions

1. Sauté onions and garlic in niter kibbeh until soft.
2. Add beef and cook until browned.
3. Season with berbere spice, salt, and pepper.
4. Simmer until beef is tender.
5. Serve hot with injera or bread.

Substitutions

- Use lamb or goat

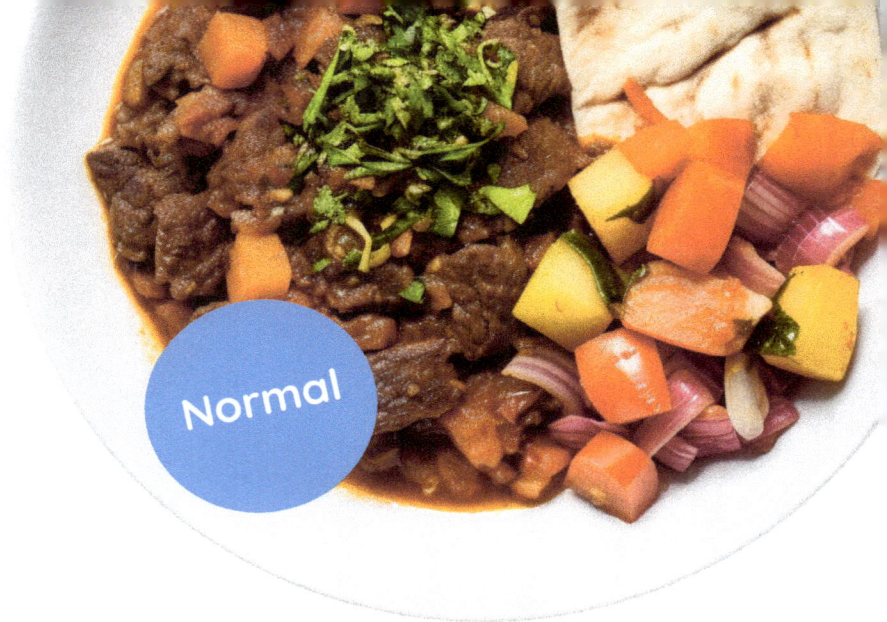

Misir Wat (Ethiopian Lentil Stew)

2 | **240 kcal** | **45**

〜〜〜〜〜〜〜

Ingredients:

- 1 cup red lentils
- 1 onion
- 2 cloves garlic
- 2 tbsp vegetable oil
- 2 tsp berbere spice
- Salt & pepper to taste

Misir Wat: A hearty Ethiopian lentil stew with a burst of flavors.

Directions

1. Boil lentils until soft, then drain.
2. Sauté onions and garlic in vegetable oil until soft.
3. Add berbere spice, salt, and pepper.
4. Mix in lentils, simmer until flavors meld.
5. Serve hot.

2   **260**   **30**

Shiro Wat (Ethiopian Chickpea Stew)

Ingredients:

- 1 cup Shiro powder
- 2 cups water
- 2 tbsp vegetable oil
- 2 cloves garlic
- Salt to taste

Normal

Shiro Wat: A luscious chickpea stew with a velvety texture, a vegan delight.

Directions

1. Mix Shiro powder with water.
2. Sauté garlic in vegetable oil until fragrant.
3. Add the Shiro mixture and simmer until thickened.
4. Season with salt.
5. Serve hot for dipping injera or bread.

2   **180**   **30**

Gomen Wat (Ethiopian Collard Greens)

Easy

Gomen Wat: Collard greens cooked to perfection in a savory sauce.

Ingredients:

- 1 bunch collard greens
- 1 onion
- 2 cloves garlic
- 2 tbsp vegetable oil
- 1 tsp turmeric
- Salt & pepper to taste

Directions

1. Wash and chop collard greens.
2. Sauté onions and garlic in vegetable oil until soft.
3. Add turmeric, salt, and pepper.
4. Cook collard greens until tender.
5. Serve hot.

Substitutions

- Use kale or spinach

2   **280**   **60**

Alicha Wot (Ethiopian Mild Stew)

Ingredients:

- 1 lb potatoes
- 2 carrots
- 2 onions
- 2 cloves garlic
- 2 tbsp vegetable oil
- 1 tsp turmeric
- Salt & pepper to taste

Easy

Alicha Wot: A mild and comforting Ethiopian stew with a delightful blend of flavors.

Directions

1. Dice potatoes and carrots.
2. Sauté onions and garlic in vegetable oil until soft.
3. Add turmeric, salt, and pepper.
4. Add potatoes and carrots, simmer until tender.
5. Serve hot.

2   **160**   **30**

Tikel Gomen (Ethiopian Cabbage Dish)

Ingredients:

- 1/2 cabbage
- 2 carrots
- 1 onion
- 2 cloves garlic
- 2 tbsp vegetable oil
- 1 tsp turmeric
- Salt & pepper to taste

Easy

Tikel Gomen: Ethiopian cabbage dish, simple yet packed with flavor.

Directions

1. Sauté onions and garlic in vegetable oil until soft.
2. Add turmeric, salt, and pepper.
3. Add chopped cabbage and carrots, cook until tender.
4. Serve hot.

2   220   45

Yekik Alicha (Ethiopian Split Pea Stew)

Ingredients:

- 1 cup yellow split peas
- 1 onion
- 2 cloves garlic
- 2 tbsp vegetable oil
- 1 tsp turmeric
- Salt & pepper to taste

Easy

Yekik Alicha: A soothing Ethiopian split pea stew, mild and satisfying.

Directions

1. Boil split peas until soft, then drain.
2. Sauté onions and garlic in vegetable oil until soft.
3. Add turmeric, salt, and pepper.
4. Mix in split peas, simmer until flavors meld.
5. Serve hot.

Substitutions

- Use red lentils

| 2 | 350 | 45 |

Doro Tibs (Ethiopian Spiced Chicken)

〰〰〰〰〰〰〰〰〰〰

Ingredients:

- 4 chicken thighs (boneless, cubed)
- 2 onions
- 2 cloves garlic
- 2 tbsp vegetable oil
- 1 tsp berbere spice
- Salt & pepper to taste

Normal

Doro Tibs: Spiced chicken stir-fry, a quick and flavorful dish.

Directions

1. Sauté onions and garlic in vegetable oil until soft.
2. Add chicken and cook until browned.
3. Season with berbere spice, salt, and pepper.
4. Serve hot with injera or bread.

Substitutions

- Use chicken breast

2   **240**   **30**

Ingudai Tibs (Ethiopian Mushroom Stir-Fry)

Easy

Ingudai Tibs: Sautéed mushrooms with Ethiopian spices, a vegetarian delight.

Ingredients:

- 2 cups mushrooms
- 1 onion
- 2 cloves garlic
- 2 tbsp olive oil
- 1 tsp paprika
- Salt & pepper to taste

Directions

1. Sauté onions and garlic in olive oil until soft.
2. Add mushrooms, cook until browned.
3. Season with paprika, salt, and pepper.
4. Serve hot with injera.

Substitutions
- Use other mushrooms

Chapter 4:
Main Courses - Meat

1   **420**   **15**

Normal

Kitfo (Ethiopian Steak Tartare)

~~~~~~~~~~~~~~~

Ingredients:

- 1/2 lb ground beef
- 1 tsp mitmita spice
- 1 tsp cardamom
- 2 tbsp niter kibbeh (spiced clarified butter)
- Injera or bread for serving
- Salt to taste

Kitfo: Raw minced beef, seasoned with spices, a bold and traditional dish.

Directions

1. Mix ground beef with mitmita spice and cardamom.
2. Sauté the beef in niter kibbeh until browned.
3. Season with salt.
4. Serve with injera or bread.

2 | 380 | 30

Tibs (Ethiopian Stir-Fried Meat)

Ingredients:

- 1/2 lb beef (cubed)
- 1 onion
- 2 cloves garlic
- 2 tbsp vegetable oil
- 1 tsp berbere spice
- Salt & pepper to taste

Normal

Tibs: Succulent meat stir-fried with vegetables and aromatic spices.

Directions

1. Sauté onions and garlic in vegetable oil until soft.
2. Add beef and cook until browned.
3. Season with berbere spice, salt, and pepper.
4. Serve hot with injera or bread.

Substitutions

- Use lamb or goat

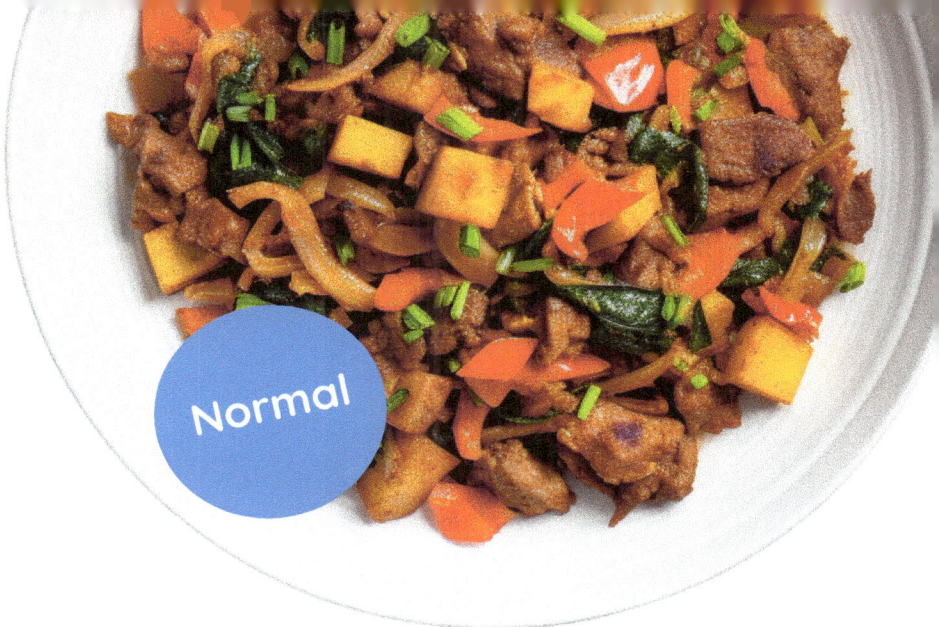

2 | **480** | **90**

Goden Tibs (Ethiopian Lamb Stew)

Ingredients:

- 1/2 lb lamb (cubed)
- 2 onions
- 4 cloves garlic
- 2 tbsp vegetable oil
- 2 tsp berbere spice
- Salt & pepper to taste

Normal

Goden Tibs: A hearty Ethiopian lamb stew with bold flavors.

Directions

1. Sauté onions and garlic in vegetable oil until soft.
2. Add lamb and cook until browned.
3. Season with berbere spice, salt, and pepper.
4. Simmer until lamb is tender.
5. Serve hot with injera or bread.

Substitutions

- Use beef

2 **420** **45**

Zilzil Tibs (Ethiopian Beef Strips)

Normal

Zilzil Tibs: Tender strips of beef marinated in Ethiopian spices and grilled.

Ingredients:

- 1/2 lb beef (sliced into strips)
- 1 onion
- 2 cloves garlic
- 2 tbsp olive oil
- 1 tsp paprika
- Salt & pepper to taste

Directions

1. Sauté onions and garlic in olive oil until soft.
2. Marinate beef with paprika, salt, and pepper.
3. Grill the beef strips until cooked to your liking.
4. Serve hot with injera or bread.

Substitutions

- Use lamb

Doro Tibs (Ethiopian Spiced Chicken)

Ingredients:

- 4 chicken thighs (boneless, cubed)
- 2 onions
- 2 cloves garlic
- 2 tbsp vegetable oil
- 1 tsp berbere spice
- Salt & pepper to taste

Doro Tibs: Spiced chicken stir-fry, a quick and flavorful dish.

Directions

1. Sauté onions and garlic in vegetable oil until soft.
2. Add chicken and cook until browned.
3. Season with berbere spice, salt, and pepper.
4. Serve hot with injera or bread.

Substitutions

- Use chicken breast

2 | **220** | **10**

Quanta Firfir (Ethiopian Beef Jerky)

Ingredients:

- 1/2 lb Quanta (Ethiopian beef jerky)
- 2 cups injera crumbs
- 2 tbsp vegetable oil
- 2 tsp berbere spice
- Salt & pepper to taste

Normal

Quanta Firfir: Spicy Ethiopian beef jerky sautéed with injera crumbs.

Directions

1. Soak Quanta in hot water until soft, then cut into strips.
2. Sauté Quanta in vegetable oil until slightly crispy.
3. Add injera crumbs and berbere spice, sauté until well mixed.
4. Season with salt and pepper.
5. Serve warm.

Substitutions

- Use beef jerky

Dulet (Ethiopian Organ Meat Stew)

mmmmmm

Ingredients:

- 1/2 lb mixed organ meats (liver, kidney, and tripe)
- 1 onion
- 2 cloves garlic
- 2 tbsp niter kibbeh (spiced clarified butter)
- 1 tsp berbere spice
- Salt & pepper to taste

Dulet: A spicy Ethiopian stew made with organ meats, not for the faint-hearted.

Directions

1. Clean and chop organ meats into small pieces.
2. Sauté onions and garlic in niter kibbeh until soft.
3. Add organ meats, berbere spice, salt, and pepper.
4. Cook until the meats are tender.
5. Serve hot.

Substitutions

- Use only liver

2 **380** **20**

Gored Gored (Ethiopian Raw Meat Dish)

Ingredients:

- 1/2 lb beef (cubed)
- 2 cloves garlic (minced)
- 1 tsp mitmita spice
- 1 tsp niter kibbeh (spiced clarified butter)
- Injera or bread for serving
- Salt to taste

Gored Gored: A unique Ethiopian dish featuring raw meat cubes, a rare delight.

Directions

1. Mix beef cubes with garlic, mitmita spice, niter kibbeh, and salt.
2. Serve immediately with injera or bread.
3. The meat should be rare in the center.
4. Enjoy the unique flavors of Gored Gored.

2   **420**   **75**

Key Wat (Ethiopian Spicy Beef Stew)

Ingredients:

- 1/2 lb beef (cubed)
- 2 onions
- 4 cloves garlic
- 2 tbsp vegetable oil
- 2 tsp berbere spice
- 2 tbsp niter kibbeh (spiced clarified butter)
- Salt & pepper to taste

Normal

Key Wat: A fiery Ethiopian beef stew that's rich in flavor and spice.

Directions

1. Sauté onions and garlic in vegetable oil until soft.
2. Add beef and cook until browned.
3. Season with berbere spice, salt, and pepper.
4. Simmer until beef is tender.
5. Add niter kibbeh for extra flavor.
6. Serve hot with injera or bread.

Substitutions

- Use lamb or goat

2 | **360** | **60**

Doro Dabo (Ethiopian Spiced Chicken)

Ingredients:

- 4 chicken drumsticks
- 2 onions
- 4 cloves garlic
- 2 tbsp berbere spice
- 2 tbsp niter kibbeh (spiced clarified butter)
- Salt & pepper to taste

Normal

Doro Dabo: A delightful Ethiopian chicken stew with aromatic spices.

Directions

1. Marinate chicken in berbere spice, garlic, and salt for 30 min.
2. Sauté onions until golden, add chicken and cook until browned.
3. Add niter kibbeh, simmer for 45 min.
4. Serve hot with injera.
5. Tear injera, scoop doro dabo, and enjoy!

Chapter 5: Main Courses - Vegetarian

2   **240**   **45**

Misir Wat (Ethiopian Lentil Stew)

Ingredients:

- 1 cup red lentils
- 1 onion
- 2 cloves garlic
- 2 tbsp vegetable oil
- 2 tsp berbere spice
- Salt & pepper to taste

Easy

Misir Wat: A hearty Ethiopian lentil stew with a burst of flavors.

Directions

1. Boil lentils until soft, then drain.
2. Sauté onions and garlic in vegetable oil until soft.
3. Add berbere spice, salt, and pepper.
4. Mix in lentils, simmer until flavors meld.
5. Serve hot.

2 **260** **30**

Shiro Wat (Ethiopian Chickpea Stew)

Ingredients:

- 1 cup Shiro powder
- 2 cups water
- 2 tbsp vegetable oil
- 2 cloves garlic
- Salt to taste

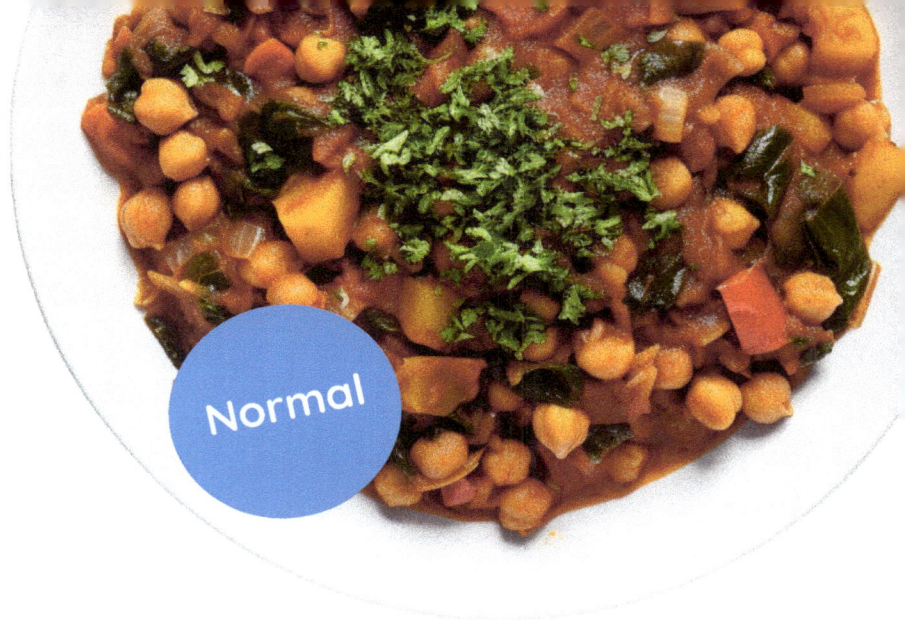

Normal

Shiro Wat: A luscious chickpea stew with a velvety texture, a vegan delight.

Directions

1. Mix Shiro powder with water.
2. Sauté garlic in vegetable oil until fragrant.
3. Add the Shiro mixture and simmer until thickened.
4. Season with salt.
5. Serve hot for dipping injera or bread.

2 | 180 | 30

Gomen Wat (Ethiopian Collard Greens)

Gomen Wat: Collard greens cooked to perfection in a savory sauce.

Ingredients:

- 1 bunch collard greens
- 1 onion
- 2 cloves garlic
- 2 tbsp vegetable oil
- 1 tsp turmeric
- Salt & pepper to taste

Directions

1. Wash and chop collard greens.
2. Sauté onions and garlic in vegetable oil until soft.
3. Add turmeric, salt, and pepper.
4. Cook collard greens until tender.
5. Serve hot.

Substitutions

- Use kale or spinach

2   **280**   **60**

Alicha Wot (Ethiopian Mild Stew)

Ingredients:

- 1 lb potatoes
- 2 carrots
- 2 onions
- 2 cloves garlic
- 2 tbsp vegetable oil
- 1 tsp turmeric
- Salt & pepper to taste

Easy

Alicha Wot: A mild and comforting Ethiopian stew with a delightful blend of flavors.

Directions

1. Dice potatoes and carrots.
2. Sauté onions and garlic in vegetable oil until soft.
3. Add turmeric, salt, and pepper.
4. Add potatoes and carrots, simmer until tender.
5. Serve hot.

2   **160**   **30**

Tikel Gomen (Ethiopian Cabbage Dish)

Ingredients:

- 1/2 cabbage
- 2 carrots
- 1 onion
- 2 cloves garlic
- 2 tbsp vegetable oil
- 1 tsp turmeric
- Salt & pepper to taste

Easy

Tikel Gomen: Ethiopian cabbage dish, simple yet packed with flavor.

Directions

1. Sauté onions and garlic in vegetable oil until soft.
2. Add turmeric, salt, and pepper.
3. Add chopped cabbage and carrots, cook until tender.
4. Serve hot.

2 **220** **45**

Yekik Alicha (Ethiopian Split Pea Stew)

Ingredients:

- 1 cup yellow split peas
- 1 onion
- 2 cloves garlic
- 2 tbsp vegetable oil
- 1 tsp turmeric
- Salt & pepper to taste

Yekik Alicha: A soothing Ethiopian split pea stew, mild and satisfying.

Directions

1. Boil split peas until soft, then drain.
2. Sauté onions and garlic in vegetable oil until soft.
3. Add turmeric, salt, and pepper.
4. Mix in split peas, simmer until flavors meld.
5. Serve hot.

Substitutions

- Use red lentils

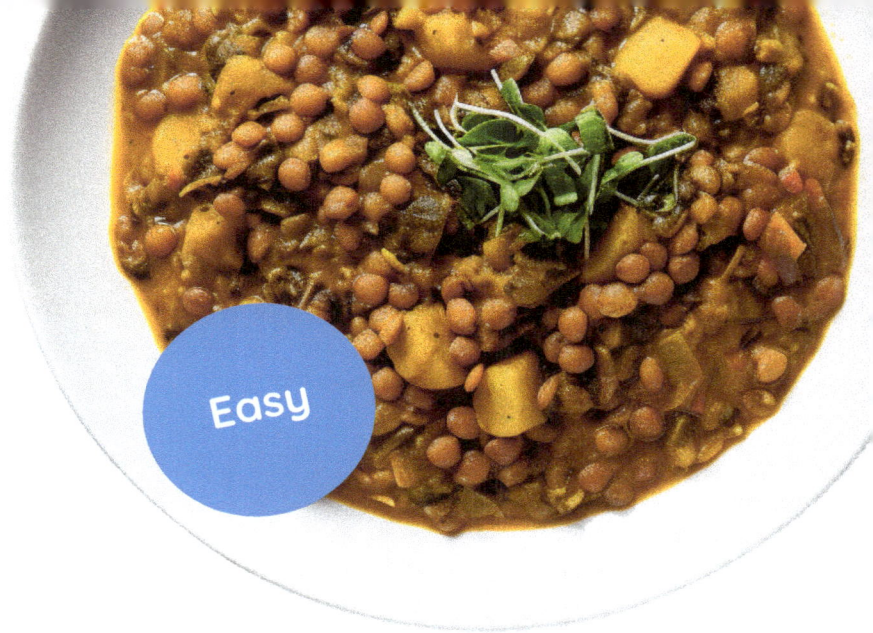

2 | **180** kcal | **25**

Easy

Fosolia (Ethiopian Green Bean Dish)

Fosolia: Ethiopian green bean dish sautéed with onions and tomatoes.

Ingredients:

- 2 cups green beans (cut into 2-inch pieces)
- 1 onion
- 2 cloves garlic
- 2 tomatoes
- 2 tbsp vegetable oil
- 1 tsp turmeric
- Salt & pepper to taste

Directions

1. Sauté onions and garlic in vegetable oil until soft.
2. Add green beans, tomatoes, turmeric, salt, and pepper.
3. Cook until beans are tender and tomatoes are soft.
4. Serve hot.

Substitutions

- Use frozen green beans

2   **160**   **15**

Buticha (Ethiopian Chickpea Dip)

Ingredients:

- 1 cup chickpea flour
- 1/4 cup plain yogurt
- 2 cloves garlic
- 2 tbsp olive oil
- 1 tsp paprika
- Salt & pepper to taste

Buticha: A creamy Ethiopian chickpea dip with a burst of flavors.

Directions

1. Mix chickpea flour with water to make a thick paste.
2. Add yogurt, garlic, olive oil, paprika, salt, and pepper.
3. Mix until smooth and creamy.
4. Serve as a dip with injera or bread.

Substitutions

- Use tahini

Ingudai Tibs (Ethiopian Mushroom Stir-Fry)

2 | **240** kcal | **30**

mmmmmmm

Ingredients:

- 2 cups mushrooms
- 1 onion
- 2 cloves garlic
- 2 tbsp olive oil
- 1 tsp paprika
- Salt & pepper to taste

Easy

Ingudai Tibs: Sautéed mushrooms with Ethiopian spices, a vegetarian delight.

Directions

1. Sauté onions and garlic in olive oil until soft.
2. Add mushrooms, cook until browned.
3. Season with paprika, salt, and pepper.
4. Serve hot with injera.

Substitutions

- Use other mushrooms

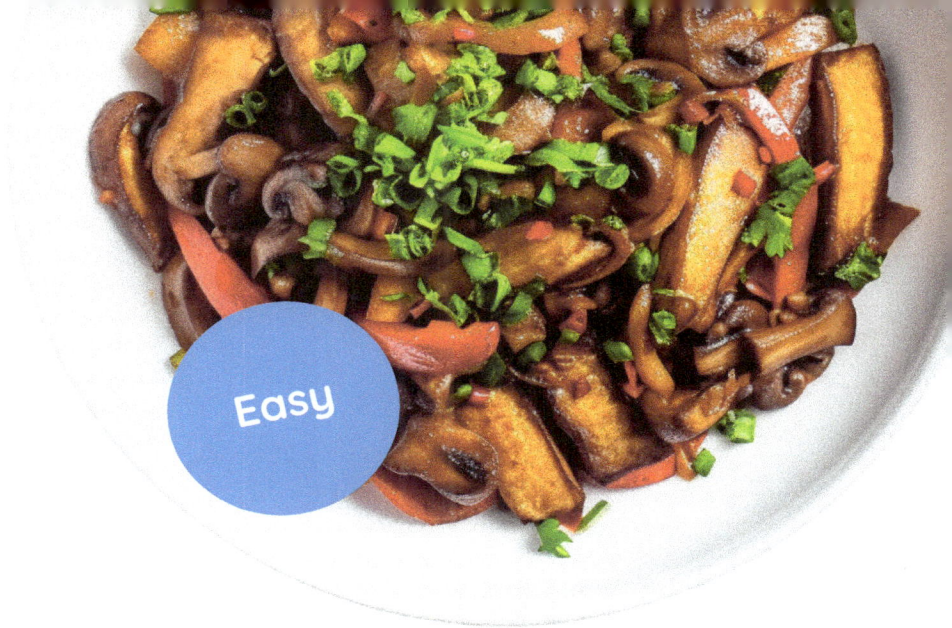

2   **180**   **30**

Azifa (Ethiopian Lentil Salad)

Ingredients:

- 1 cup green lentils
- 1/4 cup red onion
- 2 cloves garlic
- 2 tbsp olive oil
- 2 tsp Dijon mustard
- Salt & pepper to taste

Easy

Azifa: A zesty Ethiopian lentil salad with a tangy mustard vinaigrette.

Directions

1. Boil lentils until tender, then drain.
2. Mix lentils with red onion and garlic.
3. In a separate bowl, whisk together olive oil, Dijon mustard, salt, and pepper.
4. Pour the dressing over the lentil mixture and toss to coat.
5. Serve chilled.

A small favor to ask

Dear adventurous eaters and fellow culinary explorers,

As we dive into the heart and soul of Ethiopian cuisine within the pages of the "Ethiopian Comforts Cookbook: Flavors of Ethiopia - 100+ Authentic Home Comforts Made Easy for Home Cook," I want to take a moment to express my sincere appreciation for your company on this extraordinary gastronomic journey. Together, we've ventured into the vibrant world of Ethiopian flavors, bringing the rich and comforting tastes of this captivating nation to your very own kitchen.

Before we return to the tantalizing recipes that await, I have a humble request—one that carries immense significance for us as a small but passionate publishing team. In the realm of cookbooks, reviews are as precious as the most coveted spices in a seasoned chef's pantry. They are elusive, like the rhythms of Ethiopian music, yet they are the lifeblood of our creative spirit.

So, if these recipes have transported you to the bustling streets of Addis Ababa, allowing you to savor the authentic flavors of Ethiopia while making them accessible to your home kitchen, I would be eternally grateful if you could spare a moment. Please, when you have a chance, return to the app or platform where you acquired this book. There, you'll find a review button awaiting your input. A star rating and a brief sentence sharing your thoughts would be the culinary equivalent of a standing ovation in our world.

Reviews, you see, are guiding stars that light our path. They have the power to inspire other adventurous cooks to embrace Ethiopian cuisine, fostering cultural appreciation and culinary exploration.

Rest assured, every review is not just welcomed but treasured. We understand that, even in the most skilled kitchens, the most talented chefs may occasionally make a minor mistake. If you happen to spot any such hiccup along the way, please know that we've poured our hearts into this cookbook. We're human, and in the world of cooking, a touch of imperfection is part of the magic.

Now, with your indulgence, let us return to the enchanting world of Ethiopian comfort food. May the flavors of Ethiopia continue to captivate your palate, and may your culinary journey be filled with the joy of discovery and the shared delight of meals with loved ones.

Thank you for choosing the "Ethiopian Comforts Cookbook," and thank you in advance for considering leaving a review. Your support fuels our passion for creating more delectable, authentic, and accessible culinary experiences. Together, we celebrate the diverse tapestry of global cuisine, one flavorful dish at a time.

Now, let's get back to the recipes that await your eager taste buds.

Chapter 6:
Rice and Grains

2   **180**   **60**

Injera (Ethiopian Sour Flatbread)

Ingredients:

- 2 cups teff flour
- 1/2 tsp active dry yeast
- 1 1/2 cups water
- Salt to taste

Injera: Iconic Ethiopian flatbread with a unique sour flavor, perfect for scooping.

Directions

1. Mix teff flour and water in a bowl to make a batter.
2. Add yeast, cover, and let ferment for 2-3 days (until bubbly).
3. Heat a non-stick pan or injera skillet.
4. Pour a ladle of batter onto the pan, swirling to cover.
5. Cover and cook until holes form and edges lift.
6. Remove and repeat with the rest of the batter.
7. Serve injera as a delicious side or base for Ethiopian dishes.

Dabo Kolo (Ethiopian Spiced Snack)

Easy

Dabo Kolo: Crunchy, spiced Ethiopian snacks, perfect for munching.

2 | 160 | 30

Ingredients:

- 2 cups all-purpose flour
- 2 tsp berbere spice
- 1/4 cup vegetable oil
- 1/4 cup water
- Salt to taste

Directions

1. Mix flour, berbere spice, and salt.
2. Add vegetable oil and water to form a dough.
3. Roll into small balls, flatten, and cut into shapes.
4. Deep-fry until golden.
5. Let cool before munching.

Substitutions

- Use chili powder

2 | **220** | **45**

Kita (Ethiopian Flatbread)

~~~~~~~~~~~~~~~~

Ingredients:

- 2 cups all-purpose flour
- 1/2 tsp active dry yeast
- 1 cup water
- 2 tbsp vegetable oil
- Salt to taste

Substitutions

- Use whole wheat flour

Kita: A softer Ethiopian flatbread that pairs perfectly with stews.

Directions

1. Mix flour, yeast, and salt in a bowl.
2. Add water and knead into a soft dough.
3. Cover and let it rest for 30 minutes.
4. Divide into portions and roll each into a thin circle.
5. Heat a non-stick pan and brush with oil.
6. Cook each kita until puffed and lightly browned on both sides.
7. Serve warm with your favorite Ethiopian dishes.

2 **260** **90**

Ambasha (Ethiopian Sweet Bread)

Ingredients:

- 4 cups all-purpose flour
- 1/2 cup sugar
- 1/4 cup vegetable oil
- 2 tsp active dry yeast
- 1/2 cup milk
- 1/2 cup water
- 1 tsp ground cinnamon
- 1/2 tsp ground cloves
- 1/2 tsp ground nutmeg
- 1/2 tsp ground cardamom
- 1/2 tsp ground coriander
- 1/2 tsp salt

Substitutions

- Use honey or maple syrup

Normal

Ambasha: A sweet Ethiopian bread, perfect for special occasions.

Directions

1. In a bowl, mix yeast with warm water and let it proof.
2. In a separate bowl, combine flour, sugar, salt, and spices.
3. Add yeast mixture, vegetable oil, and milk. Mix well.
4. Knead the dough until smooth and elastic.
5. Cover and let it rise for 1-2 hours until doubled in size.
6. Preheat oven to 350°F (175°C).
7. Divide dough into portions and shape into round loaves.
8. Place on a baking sheet and let them rise for 30 minutes.
9. Bake for 25-30 minutes until golden brown.
10. Let cool before slicing and serving.

Taita (Ethiopian Porridge)

Ingredients:

- 1 cup cornmeal
- 4 cups water
- 1/4 cup milk
- 2 tbsp butter
- 1/4 tsp ground cinnamon
- 1/4 tsp ground cloves
- 1/4 tsp ground nutmeg
- Sugar to taste

Taita: A comforting Ethiopian porridge made with cornmeal and spices.

Directions

1. In a saucepan, bring water to a boil.
2. Slowly whisk in the cornmeal to avoid lumps.
3. Reduce heat and simmer, stirring often, until thickened.
4. Add milk, butter, and spices. Continue to cook and stir until creamy.
5. Sweeten with sugar to taste.
6. Serve warm as a comforting breakfast or snack.

Substitutions

- Use cream or coconut milk

2 **240** **60**

Kinche (Ethiopian Cracked Wheat)

mmmmmmmmm

Ingredients:

- 1 cup cracked wheat
- 2 cups water
- 1/4 cup butter
- 1/4 cup chopped onions
- 1/4 cup chopped green pepper
- 1/4 cup chopped tomatoes
- 1/4 tsp ground cumin
- 1/4 tsp ground coriander
- Salt & pepper to taste

Substitutions

- Use olive oil

Easy

Kinche: A nutritious Ethiopian dish made from cracked wheat.

Directions

1. Rinse cracked wheat and drain.
2. In a pot, sauté onions and green pepper in butter until soft.
3. Add cracked wheat, water, and spices.
4. Cook over low heat until the wheat is tender and the water is absorbed.
5. Stir in tomatoes and cook for another 5 minutes.
6. Season with salt and pepper.
7. Serve hot as a nutritious side dish or breakfast.

2   **320**   **30**

Genfo (Ethiopian Porridge)

Ingredients:

- 1 cup barley flour
- 2 cups water
- 2 tbsp niter kibbeh (spiced clarified butter)
- 1/4 tsp ground cardamom
- Salt to taste

Genfo: A hearty Ethiopian porridge made with barley and spices.

Directions

1. In a saucepan, bring water to a boil.
2. Slowly whisk in barley flour to avoid lumps.
3. Stir in niter kibbeh, cardamom, and salt.
4. Cook over low heat, stirring continuously, until thickened.
5. Serve hot in a bowl, traditionally with a well in the center filled with niter kibbeh.
6. Allow the butter to melt in the center and dip each bite into it.

Substitutions

- Use ghee or coconut oil

2   **240**   **60**

Kocho (Ethiopian Fermented Bread)

Kocho: A unique Ethiopian bread made from the Ensete plant.

Ingredients:

- 2 cups kocho flour (Ensete starch)
- 1 cup water
- Banana leaves or foil for wrapping

Directions

1. Mix kocho flour with water to form a dough.
2. Shape the dough into a flat disc.
3. Wrap the dough in banana leaves or foil.
4. Place it in a cool, dark place to ferment for at least a week, or longer for a more sour flavor.
5. Unwrap and slice the kocho.
6. Serve as a side dish with stews or dips.
7. The longer it ferments, the tangier it becomes.

Teff Pancakes (Injera Firfir)

Ingredients:

- 2 leftover injera
- 2 tbsp olive oil
- 1 onion (sliced)
- 2 cloves garlic (minced)
- 1/4 cup tomato paste
- 1/2 tsp berbere spice
- Salt to taste

Easy

Teff Pancakes (Injera Firfir): A creative way to use leftover injera.

Directions

1. Tear the leftover injera into small pieces.
2. Heat olive oil in a pan and sauté onions until soft.
3. Add garlic and cook until fragrant.
4. Stir in tomato paste, berbere spice, and salt.
5. Add the torn injera and cook until heated through.
6. Serve as a creative and flavorful breakfast or snack.

2   260   30

2 | 220 | 30

Teff Porridge (Atmit)

Ingredients:

- 1 cup teff flour
- 4 cups water
- 1/4 cup honey or maple syrup
- 1/4 tsp ground cinnamon
- 1/4 tsp ground cardamom
- 1/4 tsp salt

Easy

Teff Porridge (Atmit): A nutritious and gluten-free Ethiopian breakfast.

Directions

1. In a saucepan, whisk teff flour and water until well combined.
2. Add honey or maple syrup, cinnamon, cardamom, and salt.
3. Cook over low heat, stirring constantly, until thickened.
4. Serve warm and garnish with additional honey or syrup if desired.
5. Enjoy this gluten-free teff porridge as a nutritious breakfast or snack.

Substitutions

- Use brown sugar or agave

Chapter 7:
Breads and Pastries

2 **180** **60**

Normal

Injera (Ethiopian Sour Flatbread)

Ingredients:

- 2 cups teff flour
- 1/2 tsp active dry yeast
- 1 1/2 cups water
- Salt to taste

Injera: Iconic Ethiopian flatbread with a unique sour flavor, perfect for scooping.

Directions

1. Mix teff flour and water in a bowl to make a batter.
2. Add yeast, cover, and let ferment for 2-3 days (until bubbly).
3. Heat a non-stick pan or injera skillet.
4. Pour a ladle of batter onto the pan, swirling to cover.
5. Cover and cook until holes form and edges lift.
6. Remove and repeat with the rest of the batter.
7. Serve injera as a delicious side or base for Ethiopian dishes.

2   160   30

Dabo Kolo (Ethiopian Spiced Snack)

Easy

Dabo Kolo: Crunchy, spiced Ethiopian snacks, perfect for munching.

Ingredients:

- 2 cups all-purpose flour
- 2 tsp berbere spice
- 1/4 cup vegetable oil
- 1/4 cup water
- Salt to taste

Directions

1. Mix flour, berbere spice, and salt.
2. Add vegetable oil and water to form a dough.
3. Roll into small balls, flatten, and cut into shapes.
4. Deep-fry until golden.
5. Let cool before munching.

Substitutions

- Use chili powder

2 **220** **45**

Kita (Ethiopian Flatbread)

Ingredients:

- 2 cups all-purpose flour
- 1/2 tsp active dry yeast
- 1 cup water
- 2 tbsp vegetable oil
- Salt to taste

Kita: A softer Ethiopian flatbread that pairs perfectly with stews.

Directions

1. Mix flour, yeast, and salt in a bowl.
2. Add water and knead into a soft dough.
3. Cover and let it rest for 30 minutes.
4. Divide into portions and roll each into a thin circle.
5. Heat a non-stick pan and brush with oil.
6. Cook each kita until puffed and lightly browned on both sides.
7. Serve warm with your favorite Ethiopian dishes.

Substitutions

- Use whole wheat flour

Ambasha (Ethiopian Sweet Bread)

2   **260**   **90**

Normal

Ingredients:

- 4 cups all-purpose flour
- 1/2 cup sugar
- 1/4 cup vegetable oil
- 2 tsp active dry yeast
- 1/2 cup milk
- 1/2 cup water
- 1 tsp ground cinnamon
- 1/2 tsp ground cloves
- 1/2 tsp ground nutmeg
- 1/2 tsp ground cardamom
- 1/2 tsp ground coriander
- 1/2 tsp salt

Substitutions

- Use honey or maple syrup

Ambasha: A sweet Ethiopian bread, perfect for special occasions.

Directions

1. In a bowl, mix yeast with warm water and let it proof.
2. In a separate bowl, combine flour, sugar, salt, and spices.
3. Add yeast mixture, vegetable oil, and milk. Mix well.
4. Knead the dough until smooth and elastic.
5. Cover and let it rise for 1-2 hours until doubled in size.
6. Preheat oven to 350°F (175°C).
7. Divide dough into portions and shape into round loaves.
8. Place on a baking sheet and let them rise for 30 minutes.
9. Bake for 25-30 minutes until golden brown.
10. Let cool before slicing and serving.

2 **200** **30**

Taita (Ethiopian Porridge)

Easy

Ingredients:

- 1 cup cornmeal
- 4 cups water
- 1/4 cup milk
- 2 tbsp butter
- 1/4 tsp ground cinnamon
- 1/4 tsp ground cloves
- 1/4 tsp ground nutmeg
- Sugar to taste

Taita: A comforting Ethiopian porridge made with cornmeal and spices.

Directions

1. In a saucepan, bring water to a boil.
2. Slowly whisk in the cornmeal to avoid lumps.
3. Reduce heat and simmer, stirring often, until thickened.
4. Add milk, butter, and spices. Continue to cook and stir until creamy.
5. Sweeten with sugar to taste.
6. Serve warm as a comforting breakfast or snack.

Substitutions

- Use cream or coconut milk

2   **320**   **30**

Genfo (Ethiopian Porridge)

Normal

Genfo: A hearty Ethiopian porridge made with barley and spices.

Ingredients:

- 1 cup barley flour
- 2 cups water
- 2 tbsp niter kibbeh (spiced clarified butter)
- 1/4 tsp ground cardamom
- Salt to taste

Directions

1. In a saucepan, bring water to a boil.
2. Slowly whisk in barley flour to avoid lumps.
3. Stir in niter kibbeh, cardamom, and salt.
4. Cook over low heat, stirring continuously, until thickened.
5. Serve hot in a bowl, traditionally with a well in the center filled with niter kibbeh.
6. Allow the butter to melt in the center and dip each bite into it.

Substitutions

- Use ghee or coconut oil

2   **240**   **60**

Kocho (Ethiopian Fermented Bread)

Normal

Kocho: A unique Ethiopian bread made from the Ensete plant.

Ingredients:

- 2 cups kocho flour (Ensete starch)
- 1 cup water
- Banana leaves or foil for wrapping

Directions

1. Mix kocho flour with water to form a dough.
2. Shape the dough into a flat disc.
3. Wrap the dough in banana leaves or foil.
4. Place it in a cool, dark place to ferment for at least a week, or longer for a more sour flavor.
5. Unwrap and slice the kocho.
6. Serve as a side dish with stews or dips.
7. The longer it ferments, the tangier it becomes.

Substitutions

- None

2 **260** **30**

Teff Pancakes (Injera Firfir)

Ingredients:

- 2 leftover injera
- 2 tbsp olive oil
- 1 onion (sliced)
- 2 cloves garlic (minced)
- 1/4 cup tomato paste
- 1/2 tsp berbere spice
- Salt to taste

Substitutions

- None

Easy

Teff Pancakes (Injera Firfir): A creative way to use leftover injera.

Directions

1. Tear the leftover injera into small pieces.
2. Heat olive oil in a pan and sauté onions until soft.
3. Add garlic and cook until fragrant.
4. Stir in tomato paste, berbere spice, and salt.
5. Add the torn injera and cook until heated through.
6. Serve as a creative and flavorful breakfast or snack.

2   **220**   **30**

Teff Porridge (Atmit)

Ingredients:

- 1 cup teff flour
- 4 cups water
- 1/4 cup honey or maple syrup
- 1/4 tsp ground cinnamon
- 1/4 tsp ground cardamom
- 1/4 tsp salt

Substitutions

- Use brown sugar or agave

Easy

Teff Porridge (Atmit): A nutritious and gluten-free Ethiopian breakfast.

Directions

1. In a saucepan, whisk teff flour and water until well combined.
2. Add honey or maple syrup, cinnamon, cardamom, and salt.
3. Cook over low heat, stirring constantly, until thickened.
4. Serve warm and garnish with additional honey or syrup if desired.
5. Enjoy this gluten-free teff porridge as a nutritious breakfast or snack.

2   260   90

Hambasha (Ethiopian Communion Bread)

Ingredients:

- 4 cups all-purpose flour
- 1/4 cup sugar
- 2 tsp active dry yeast
- 1/4 cup vegetable oil
- 1/4 cup milk
- 1/2 cup water
- 1/4 tsp ground cardamom
- 1/4 tsp ground coriander
- 1/4 tsp ground nutmeg
- 1/4 tsp ground cloves
- 1/4 tsp salt

Substitutions

- Use honey or maple syrup

Normal

Hambasha: A sacred Ethiopian bread traditionally used in religious ceremonies.

Directions

1. In a bowl, mix yeast with warm water and let it proof.
2. In a separate bowl, combine flour, sugar, salt, and spices.
3. Add yeast mixture, vegetable oil, and milk. Mix well.
4. Knead the dough until smooth and elastic.
5. Cover and let it rise for 1-2 hours until doubled in size.
6. Preheat oven to 350°F (175°C).
7. Divide dough into portions and shape into round loaves.
8. Place on a baking sheet and let them rise for 30 minutes.
9. Bake for 25-30 minutes until golden brown.
10. Let cool before slicing and serving.

Chapter 8: Desserts - Cakes and Sweets

2 | **320** kcal | **60**

Ethiopian Honey Bread (Yemarina Yewotet Dabo)

Ingredients:

- 3 cups all-purpose flour
- 2 tsp active dry yeast
- 1/4 cup honey
- 1/4 cup vegetable oil
- 1/2 cup warm water
- 1/2 tsp ground cinnamon
- 1/2 tsp ground cloves
- 1/2 tsp ground nutmeg
- 1/2 tsp ground cardamom
- 1/2 tsp salt

Substitutions

- Use brown sugar or maple syrup

Normal

Ethiopian Honey Bread (Yemarina Yewotet Dabo): A sweet, fragrant bread with a touch of honey.

Directions

1. In a bowl, dissolve yeast in warm water and let it proof.
2. In a separate bowl, mix flour, honey, salt, and spices.
3. Add yeast mixture and vegetable oil. Mix until it forms a dough.
4. Knead until smooth and elastic.
5. Cover and let it rise for 1-2 hours until doubled in size.
6. Preheat oven to 350°F (175°C).
7. Divide dough into portions and shape into a round loaf or braided bread.
8. Place on a baking sheet and let it rise for 30 minutes.
9. Bake for 25-30 minutes until golden brown.
10. Let cool before slicing and serving.

2 | **240** | **60**

Ethiopian Banana Bread (Dabo Na Banana)

Normal

Ethiopian Banana Bread (Dabo Na Banana): Moist and flavorful banana bread with an Ethiopian twist.

Ingredients:

- 2 cups all-purpose flour
- 1 tsp baking powder
- 1/2 tsp baking soda
- 1/2 tsp salt
- 1/2 cup unsalted butter (room temperature)
- 1 cup granulated sugar
- 2 large eggs
- 3 ripe bananas (mashed)
- 1/4 cup plain yogurt
- 1 tsp vanilla extract
- 1/2 tsp ground cinnamon
- 1/2 tsp ground cardamom

Substitutions

- Use whole wheat flour

Directions

1. Preheat oven to 350°F (175°C). Grease and flour a loaf pan.
2. In a bowl, whisk together flour, baking powder, baking soda, and salt.
3. In another bowl, cream butter and sugar until light and fluffy.
4. Beat in eggs, one at a time, then stir in mashed bananas, yogurt, vanilla extract, and spices.
5. Gradually add dry ingredients and mix until just combined.
6. Pour batter into the prepared loaf pan.
7. Bake for 60-65 minutes or until a toothpick inserted into the center comes out clean.
8. Let cool before slicing and serving.

2 | **120** | **15**

Ethiopian Fruit Salad

Ingredients:

- 2 oranges (peeled and segmented)
- 2 bananas (sliced)
- 1 cup grapes (halved)
- 1 apple (diced)
- 1 pear (diced)
- 1/4 cup fresh pineapple (diced)
- Juice of 1 lemon
- 2 tbsp honey
- 1/2 tsp ground cinnamon

Substitutions

- Use lime juice

Easy

Ethiopian Fruit Salad: A refreshing and colorful salad with a citrusy kick.

Directions

1. In a large bowl, combine all the fruits.
2. In a small bowl, whisk together lemon juice, honey, and ground cinnamon.
3. Drizzle the dressing over the fruit salad and gently toss to coat.
4. Chill in the refrigerator for at least 30 minutes before serving.
5. Enjoy this vibrant and tangy fruit salad as a dessert or a refreshing side dish.

2   **150**   **240**

Ethiopian Mango Sorbet (Amashaza)

Ingredients:

- 2 ripe mangoes (peeled, pitted, and diced)
- 1/2 cup sugar
- Juice of 1 lime
- 1/2 tsp ground cardamom
- Pinch of salt

Substitutions

- Use orange juice

Normal

Ethiopian Mango Sorbet (Amashaza): A cool and tropical treat made from ripe mangoes.

Directions

1. Place diced mangoes in a blender or food processor.
2. Add sugar, lime juice, ground cardamom, and a pinch of salt.
3. Blend until smooth.
4. Transfer the mixture to a shallow, freezer-safe dish.
5. Cover and freeze for at least 4 hours, or until firm.
6. Before serving, let the sorbet sit at room temperature for a few minutes to soften slightly.
7. Scoop and enjoy this delightful mango sorbet as a refreshing dessert.

2 | 350 kcal | 60

Normal

Ethiopian Chocolate Cake

munnunnunn

Ingredients:

- 1 3/4 cups all-purpose flour
- 1 1/2 tsp baking powder
- 1 1/2 tsp baking soda
- 1/2 cup unsweetened cocoa powder
- 1 1/2 cups granulated sugar
- 2 eggs
- 1 cup buttermilk
- 1/2 cup vegetable oil
- 1 tsp vanilla extract
- 1 cup strong brewed Ethiopian coffee (cooled)
- Pinch of salt
- Butter and flour for greasing and dusting the pan
- Powdered sugar for dusting (optional)

Substitutions

- Use dark chocolate cocoa powder

Ethiopian Chocolate Cake: A rich and decadent dessert with Ethiopian flair.

Directions

1. Preheat oven to 350°F (175°C). Grease and flour a cake pan.
2. In a bowl, whisk together flour, cocoa powder, baking powder, baking soda, and a pinch of salt.
3. In another bowl, beat eggs and sugar until light and fluffy.
4. Stir in buttermilk, vegetable oil, and vanilla extract.
5. Gradually add dry ingredients and mix until smooth.
6. Stir in brewed coffee.
7. Pour batter into the prepared cake pan.
8. Bake for 30-35 minutes or until a toothpick inserted into the center comes out clean.
9. Let the cake cool in the pan for 10 minutes before transferring to a wire rack to cool completely.
10. Dust with powdered sugar if desired.
11. Slice and savor this luscious Ethiopian chocolate cake.

2 **180** **45**

Atmit (Ethiopian Teff Pudding)

Ingredients:

- 1/2 cup teff flour
- 2 cups milk
- 1/4 cup sugar
- 1/2 tsp ground cinnamon
- 1/2 tsp ground cardamom
- 1/4 tsp salt
- 1/4 cup chopped nuts (e.g., almonds, walnuts)
- 1/4 cup raisins
- 1/2 tsp vanilla extract

Substitutions

- Use honey or maple syrup

Easy

Atmit (Ethiopian Teff Pudding): A creamy and nutty pudding made from teff flour.

Directions

1. In a saucepan, whisk teff flour and milk until well combined.
2. Add sugar, ground cinnamon, ground cardamom, and salt.
3. Cook over low heat, stirring constantly, until thickened.
4. Remove from heat and stir in chopped nuts, raisins, and vanilla extract.
5. Transfer to serving bowls or glasses.
6. Let it cool and set in the refrigerator for at least 30 minutes before serving.
7. Enjoy this creamy and nutty teff pudding as a delightful dessert.

Ethiopian Sesame Candy (Sima)

2 | 180 | 30

~~~~~~~~~~~~~~~~~~~~~

Ingredients:

- 1 cup sesame seeds
- 1/2 cup honey
- 1/4 cup sugar
- 1/4 tsp ground cardamom
- 1/4 tsp ground cinnamon
- Pinch of salt

Substitutions

- Use agave syrup or maple syrup

Normal

Ethiopian Sesame Candy (Sima): A delightful and nutty sweet treat.

Directions

1. In a dry skillet, toast sesame seeds over medium heat until golden brown and fragrant. Remove and set aside.
2. In a saucepan, combine honey, sugar, ground cardamom, ground cinnamon, and a pinch of salt.
3. Cook over low heat, stirring constantly, until the mixture reaches 260°F (127°C) on a candy thermometer (hard-ball stage).
4. Remove from heat and quickly stir in toasted sesame seeds.
5. Pour the mixture onto a greased and parchment-lined baking sheet. Flatten with a spatula.
6. Let it cool and set for about 30 minutes, then break it into pieces.
7. Enjoy this crunchy and nutty Ethiopian sesame candy.

2   **240**   **60**

Ethiopian Rice Pudding (Atar Allecha)

Ingredients:

- 1/2 cup Arborio rice
- 2 cups milk
- 1/4 cup sugar
- 1/4 tsp ground cardamom
- 1/4 tsp ground cinnamon
- 1/4 tsp ground cloves
- 1/4 tsp ground nutmeg
- Pinch of salt
- 1/4 cup golden raisins
- 1/4 cup chopped almonds
- 1/2 tsp vanilla extract

Substitutions

- Use cashews or pistachios

Easy

Ethiopian Rice Pudding (Atar Allecha): A creamy and comforting dessert with a hint of spice.

Directions

1. In a saucepan, combine rice, milk, sugar, ground cardamom, ground cinnamon, ground cloves, ground nutmeg, and a pinch of salt.
2. Bring to a simmer over medium heat, stirring frequently.
3. Reduce heat to low and continue to simmer, stirring often, until the rice is tender and the mixture thickens (about 30 minutes).
4. Stir in golden raisins, chopped almonds, and vanilla extract.
5. Cook for an additional 5 minutes until the raisins plump up.
6. Remove from heat and let it cool for a few minutes before serving.
7. Enjoy this creamy and spiced Ethiopian rice pudding.

Icons: 2 | kcal 160 | 60

Ethiopian Date Bread (Dabo Kolo)

Ingredients:

- 2 cups all-purpose flour
- 1/2 cup sugar
- 1/2 cup unsalted butter
- 1/4 cup milk
- 1/2 cup chopped dates
- 1/2 tsp baking powder
- 1/4 tsp ground cinnamon
- 1/4 tsp ground cardamom
- 1/4 tsp ground cloves
- 1/4 tsp salt
- Powdered sugar for dusting (optional)

Substitutions

- Use whole wheat flour

Ethiopian Date Bread (Dabo Kolo): Sweet and chewy bites of date goodness.

Directions

1. Preheat oven to 350°F (175°C). Grease and flour a baking sheet or line it with parchment paper.
2. In a bowl, cream together sugar and unsalted butter until fluffy.
3. Stir in milk, chopped dates, and spices.
4. In another bowl, whisk together flour, baking powder, and salt.
5. Gradually add dry ingredients to the wet mixture and mix until a dough forms.
6. Shape the dough into small balls or rolls.
7. Place them on the prepared baking sheet.
8. Bake for 20-25 minutes or until golden brown.
9. Let cool and dust with powdered sugar if desired.
10. Enjoy these sweet and chewy Ethiopian date bread bites.

Normal

2   220   45

Ethiopian Nut Bars (Tosho)

~~~~~~~~~~~~~~~~~~~~~~~~~~~~~

Ingredients:

- 1 1/2 cups mixed nuts (e.g., almonds, walnuts, peanuts, cashews)
- 1/2 cup sugar
- 1/4 cup unsalted butter
- 1/4 cup water
- 1/2 tsp ground cardamom
- 1/2 tsp ground cinnamon
- 1/4 tsp salt

Substitutions

- Use honey or maple syrup

Ethiopian Nut Bars (Tosho): Crunchy and nutty bars with a touch of sweetness.

Directions

1. Preheat oven to 350°F (175°C). Grease and line a baking pan with parchment paper.
2. In a food processor, pulse the mixed nuts until coarsely chopped.
3. In a saucepan, combine sugar, unsalted butter, water, ground cardamom, ground cinnamon, and salt.
4. Cook over low heat, stirring constantly, until the mixture thickens and turns golden brown (about 5-7 minutes).
5. Remove from heat and stir in the chopped nuts.
6. Pour the mixture into the prepared baking pan.
7. Press it down evenly with a spatula.
8. Bake for 20-25 minutes or until golden brown and set.
9. Let cool in the pan before cutting into bars.
10. Enjoy these crunchy and nutty Ethiopian nut bars as a delightful snack.

Chapter 9:
Desserts - Fruits and Nuts

1 cup   120   10

Ethiopian Mango Sorbet (Amashaza)

Easy

Ingredients:

- 2 ripe mangoes (peeled and cubed)
- 1/4 cup sugar
- 1/4 cup water
- Juice of 1 lime
- Zest of 1 lime
- Pinch of salt

Indulge in the sweet, tropical flavors of Ethiopia with Amashaza, a delightful mango sorbet that's perfect for hot days. Legend has it that this recipe was a favorite of Emperor Haile Selassie, who couldn't resist its cool, fruity embrace.

Directions

1. In a saucepan, combine sugar and water. Heat over medium heat until the sugar dissolves, then let it simmer for 2 minutes to create a simple syrup. Let it cool.
2. In a blender, add the ripe mango cubes, lime juice, lime zest, and a pinch of salt. Blend until smooth.
3. Pour the mango mixture into a bowl and stir in the cooled simple syrup.
4. Pour the mixture into an ice cream maker and churn according to the manufacturer's instructions.
5. Transfer the sorbet to an airtight container and freeze for at least 4 hours before serving.
6. Scoop into bowls, garnish with lime zest, and enjoy your Amashaza Mango Sorbet!

Substitutions

- You can use honey instead of sugar for a different sweetness.
- Try adding a splash of rum for an adult twist.
- If you don't have an ice cream maker, freeze the mixture in a shallow dish, stirring every hour until it's firm.
- For a creamier texture, add a dollop of yogurt before churning.

1 cup   80   15

Ethiopian Fruit Salad

~~~~~~~~~~~~

Ingredients:

- 1 ripe papaya (cubed)
- 1 ripe mango (cubed)
- 1 cup pineapple chunks
- 1 cup seedless grapes
- 1 orange (peeled and segmented)
- 1 tablespoon honey
- Juice of 1 lime
- Pinch of ground cinnamon
- Fresh mint leaves for garnish

Super Easy

This refreshing fruit salad brings together the vibrant flavors of Ethiopia. A traditional treat enjoyed during celebrations, it's a burst of colors and tastes that dance on your palate.

Directions

1. In a large bowl, combine all the fruit pieces.
2. Drizzle honey and lime juice over the fruit.
3. Sprinkle a pinch of ground cinnamon for a hint of warmth.
4. Gently toss the fruit salad until well coated.
5. Garnish with fresh mint leaves.
6. Chill in the fridge for 30 minutes before serving.
7. Enjoy the explosion of flavors in your Ethiopian Fruit Salad!

Substitutions

- Feel free to use your favorite fruits or whatever is in season.
- Swap honey with agave syrup for a vegan option.
- Add a dash of chili powder for a spicy twist.
- For extra crunch, sprinkle some toasted coconut on top.

1 slice   **150**   **60**

Ethiopian Banana Bread (Dabo Na Banana)

Normal

Ingredients:

- 2 overripe bananas (mashed)
- 1/2 cup sugar
- 1/4 cup butter (melted)
- 1 egg
- 1 1/2 cups all-purpose flour
- 1 teaspoon baking soda
- 1/2 teaspoon salt
- 1/2 teaspoon ground cinnamon
- 1/4 teaspoon ground nutmeg
- 1/4 teaspoon ground cloves
- 1/2 cup chopped walnuts (optional)

Dabo Na Banana, a beloved Ethiopian dessert, combines the richness of ripe bananas with warm spices. It's like a cozy hug for your taste buds.

Directions

1. Preheat your oven to 350°F (175°C). Grease and flour a loaf pan.
2. In a bowl, mix mashed bananas, sugar, melted butter, and egg until well combined.
3. In another bowl, whisk together flour, baking soda, salt, and spices.
4. Combine the wet and dry ingredients until just incorporated. Fold in the chopped walnuts if using.
5. Pour the batter into the prepared loaf pan.
6. Bake for 45-55 minutes, or until a toothpick inserted into the center comes out clean.
7. Allow the banana bread to cool before slicing and savoring each delightful bite.

Substitutions

- Replace walnuts with chocolate chips for a sweeter twist.
- Use coconut oil instead of butter for a tropical flavor.
- Add a handful of raisins for extra sweetness and texture.
- Serve with a dollop of whipped cream for an indulgent treat.

2 pieces   **60**   **20**

Ethiopian Sesame Candy (Sima)

Ingredients:

- 1 cup sesame seeds
- 1/2 cup honey
- 1/4 cup sugar
- 1/4 teaspoon ground cardamom
- Pinch of salt

Sima, the Ethiopian sesame candy, is a crunchy delight with a hint of sweetness. It's a favorite snack enjoyed during coffee ceremonies and family gatherings.

Directions

1. Toast the sesame seeds in a dry skillet over medium heat until golden brown. Remove from heat and set aside.
2. In a saucepan, combine honey, sugar, ground cardamom, and a pinch of salt.
3. Cook over medium-low heat, stirring continuously, until the mixture reaches 280°F (140°C) on a candy thermometer.
4. Remove from heat and quickly stir in the toasted sesame seeds.
5. Pour the mixture onto a greased baking sheet and flatten it with a spatula.
6. Let it cool and harden for about 15 minutes, then break it into pieces.
7. Enjoy your homemade Sima sesame candy!

Substitutions

- Add crushed pistachios for a nutty variation.
- Replace cardamom with cinnamon for a different flavor profile.
- Experiment with different honey varieties for unique tastes.
- Store in an airtight container to maintain freshness.

1/2 cup   **120**   **30**

Ethiopian Roasted Chickpeas

~~~~~~~~~~~~~~~~

Ingredients:

- 1 can (15 oz) chickpeas, drained and rinsed
- 2 tablespoons olive oil
- 1 teaspoon berbere spice blend (or paprika for milder flavor)
- 1/2 teaspoon salt
- 1/2 teaspoon garlic powder
- 1/2 teaspoon onion powder

Substitutions

- Customize the spice blend to your preference for more heat or smokiness.
- Try different seasonings like cumin and chili powder for variety.
- Add a squeeze of fresh lemon juice for a zesty twist.
- Store in an airtight container to keep them crunchy.

Super Easy

These savory roasted chickpeas are a popular Ethiopian snack. They're crispy, flavorful, and the perfect munchies for any occasion.

Directions

1. Preheat your oven to 400°F (200°C).
2. Rinse and drain chickpeas, then pat them dry with a paper towel.
3. In a bowl, toss chickpeas with olive oil, berbere spice (or paprika), salt, garlic powder, and onion powder until evenly coated.
4. Spread chickpeas on a baking sheet in a single layer.
5. Roast in the oven for 25-30 minutes, stirring once or twice, until they're crispy and golden.
6. Let them cool slightly before devouring your Ethiopian Roasted Chickpeas!

2 tablespoons

90 kcal

15

Easy

Ethiopian Peanut Butter

mmmmmmmmm

Ingredients:

- 2 cups roasted peanuts
- 1/4 cup honey
- 1/4 teaspoon salt
- 1/4 teaspoon ground cinnamon (optional)
- 1/4 teaspoon ground cardamom (optional)

Homemade Ethiopian peanut butter is a creamy delight with a touch of sweetness. Spread it on injera or toast for a traditional treat that's both nostalgic and delicious.

Directions

1. Place roasted peanuts in a food processor.
2. Blend for a few minutes until the peanuts turn into a thick paste.
3. Add honey, salt, and optional spices if desired.
4. Continue blending until everything is well combined and smooth.
5. Taste and adjust sweetness and seasoning as needed.
6. Transfer your homemade peanut butter to a jar and refrigerate.
7. Spread on injera, toast, or enjoy as a dip!

Substitutions

- Use maple syrup for a different sweetness.
- Experiment with other spices like nutmeg or cloves for unique flavors.
- Add a pinch of salt for a savory twist.
- For extra creaminess, drizzle in a bit of coconut oil.

10 pieces · **110** kcal · **45**

Ethiopian Date Bread (Dabo Kolo)

~~~~~~~~~~~~~~~~~~~~

Normal

Dabo Kolo, or Ethiopian date bread, is a delightful snack perfect for tea time. These bite-sized treats are both sweet and satisfying, with a hint of spice.

Ingredients:

- 1 cup all-purpose flour
- 1/4 cup sugar
- 1/4 cup butter (room temperature)
- 1/4 cup dates (chopped)
- 1/4 teaspoon ground cardamom
- 1/4 teaspoon ground cloves
- 1/4 teaspoon baking powder
- Pinch of salt
- 2 tablespoons water

Directions

1. Preheat your oven to 350°F (175°C).
2. In a bowl, cream together sugar and butter until fluffy.
3. Add chopped dates and mix well.
4. In another bowl, whisk together flour, cardamom, cloves, baking powder, and a pinch of salt.
5. Gradually add the dry ingredients to the date mixture, mixing until a dough forms. Add water if needed to make it pliable.
6. Divide the dough into small balls and shape them into rings or sticks.
7. Place them on a baking sheet and bake for 15-20 minutes, or until they're lightly golden.
8. Let them cool before enjoying your Dabo Kolo!

Substitutions

- Substitute dates with raisins for a different fruity flavor.
- Add a dash of ground ginger for extra spice.
- Drizzle with honey for a touch of sweetness after baking.
- Store in an airtight container to keep them fresh.

1 bar   **180**   **25**

Easy

Ethiopian Nut Bars (Tosho)

Ingredients:

- 1 cup mixed nuts (almonds, cashews, peanuts, etc.)
- 1/2 cup honey
- 1/4 cup peanut butter
- 1/4 cup dried fruits (raisins, apricots, etc.)
- 1/4 cup shredded coconut
- 1/4 teaspoon ground cinnamon
- Pinch of salt

Tosho, the Ethiopian nut bars, are a crunchy delight packed with protein and flavor. These bars are perfect for a quick energy boost during your busy day.

Directions

1. In a food processor, pulse the mixed nuts until coarsely chopped.
2. In a saucepan, warm honey and peanut butter over low heat until well combined.
3. Stir in dried fruits, shredded coconut, ground cinnamon, and a pinch of salt.
4. Mix in the chopped nuts until evenly distributed.
5. Line a baking dish with parchment paper and press the mixture firmly into it.
6. Refrigerate for at least 2 hours until set.
7. Cut into bars and enjoy your homemade Tosho Nut Bars!

Substitutions

- Customize the nut blend to your preference.
- Swap peanut butter for almond or cashew butter for a different flavor.
- Experiment with different dried fruits for variety.
- Drizzle with melted chocolate for an extra treat.

1 cup   100   15

Ethiopian Orange Sorbet

Ingredients:

- 2 cups fresh orange juice (from about 4 oranges)
- 1/2 cup sugar
- 1/2 cup water
- Zest of 1 orange
- Juice of 1 lemon
- Pinch of salt

Substitutions

- Add a splash of orange liqueur for an adult twist.
- Garnish with fresh mint leaves for extra freshness.
- For a creamy variation, blend in some Greek yogurt before churning.
- Use honey instead of sugar for a different sweetness.

Experience the zesty freshness of Ethiopian oranges in this delightful sorbet. It's a citrusy symphony that will brighten up your day.

Directions

1. In a saucepan, combine sugar, water, and a pinch of salt. Heat over medium heat until the sugar dissolves, then let it simmer for 2 minutes to create a simple syrup. Let it cool.
2. In a bowl, mix fresh orange juice, orange zest, and lemon juice.
3. Stir in the cooled simple syrup.
4. Pour the mixture into an ice cream maker and churn according to the manufacturer's instructions.
5. Transfer the sorbet to an airtight container and freeze for at least 4 hours before serving.
6. Scoop into bowls and savor the tangy delight of Ethiopian Orange Sorbet!

2 pieces **90** kcal **30**

Ethiopian Coconut Candies

~~~~~~~~~~

Super Easy

These sweet coconut candies are a beloved Ethiopian treat. They're bite-sized bursts of coconut goodness with a hint of cardamom.

Ingredients:

- 2 cups shredded coconut
- 1/2 cup sweetened condensed milk
- 1/4 teaspoon ground cardamom
- 1/4 teaspoon vanilla extract
- Pinch of salt
- Unsweetened cocoa powder for dusting (optional)

Directions

1. In a bowl, combine shredded coconut, sweetened condensed milk, ground cardamom, vanilla extract, and a pinch of salt.
2. Mix until the ingredients come together into a sticky dough.
3. Form small, bite-sized balls or shapes from the dough.
4. If desired, roll the candies in unsweetened cocoa powder for an extra layer of flavor.
5. Place them on a parchment-lined tray and refrigerate for about 30 minutes until firm.
6. Enjoy your homemade Ethiopian Coconut Candies!

Substitutions

- Add finely chopped nuts for a crunchy texture.
- Replace cardamom with cinnamon for a different spice profile.
- Drizzle with melted chocolate for a decadent touch.
- Store in the refrigerator to keep them fresh.

Chapter 10:
Beverages

1 cup   5   10

Ethiopian Coffee (Bunna)

Ingredients:

- 2 tablespoons finely ground Ethiopian coffee beans
- 1 cup water
- Sugar (optional)
- Spices like cinnamon or cardamom (optional)
- A traditional coffee pot called a "jebena" (or substitute with a small saucepan)
- Jebena/Moka pot for brewing (or a standard coffee maker)
- A heat source (stove or coffee maker)

Substitutions

- Adjust the coffee-to-water ratio for your preferred strength.
- Experiment with different Ethiopian coffee bean varieties for unique flavors.
- Use a standard coffee maker if you don't have a jebena.
- Add a dash of milk or cream for a creamy twist.

Normal

Experience the rich tradition of Ethiopian coffee, Bunna, in the comfort of your home. It's not just a beverage; it's a cultural ritual that brings people together.

Directions

1. In a jebena or small saucepan, bring 1 cup of water to a simmer.
2. Add finely ground coffee beans to the simmering water.
3. Let it simmer for a few minutes, stirring occasionally.
4. Remove from heat when the coffee forms a foam at the surface.
5. Allow the grounds to settle for a moment.
6. Pour the brewed coffee into cups, leaving the grounds behind.
7. Sweeten to taste with sugar if desired, and add spices if you like.
8. Enjoy the authentic Ethiopian Bunna experience with friends and family!

Ethiopian Tea (Shai)

Super Easy

1 cup | **10 kcal** | **5**

Sip on the soothing flavors of Ethiopian Shai tea. It's a simple yet comforting brew enjoyed throughout the day, often with a touch of sugar and a side of conversation.

Ingredients:

- 1 black tea bag (Ethiopian or your choice)
- 1 cup boiling water
- Sugar or honey (to taste)
- Milk (optional)
- A pinch of ground cloves (optional)
- A pinch of ground cinnamon (optional)
- A sprig of fresh mint (for garnish, optional)

Directions

1. Place a tea bag in a cup.
2. Pour boiling water over the tea bag.
3. Let it steep for 3-5 minutes, or until it reaches your desired strength.
4. Remove the tea bag and discard it.
5. Sweeten with sugar or honey to taste.
6. Add milk if desired for a creamy texture.
7. Sprinkle ground cloves and cinnamon for extra flavor if you like.
8. Garnish with a sprig of fresh mint if available.
9. Sip and savor the warmth of Ethiopian Shai tea.

Substitutions

- Use your favorite tea variety, such as Earl Grey or green tea, for a different flavor.
- Experiment with different sweeteners like agave syrup or stevia.
- Adjust the steeping time to control the strength of the tea.
- Try it iced for a refreshing twist.

1 cup | 15 kcal | 15

Ethiopian Spiced Tea (Ataya)

Easy

Ingredients:

- 1 black tea bag (Ethiopian or your choice)
- 1 cup boiling water
- Sugar or honey (to taste)
- Ground cinnamon
- Ground cloves
- A pinch of ground ginger (optional)
- A pinch of ground nutmeg (optional)
- A sprig of fresh mint (for garnish, optional)

Ataya, the Ethiopian spiced tea, is a warm and fragrant concoction infused with spices like cinnamon and cloves. It's perfect for chilly evenings and gatherings with loved ones.

Directions

1. Place a tea bag in a cup.
2. Pour boiling water over the tea bag.
3. Let it steep for 3-5 minutes, or until it reaches your desired strength.
4. Remove the tea bag and discard it.
5. Sweeten with sugar or honey to taste.
6. Add a pinch of ground cinnamon, cloves, and optional ginger and nutmeg for a spicy kick.
7. Garnish with a sprig of fresh mint if available.
8. Sip and enjoy the comforting embrace of Ethiopian Ataya spiced tea.

Substitutions

- Customize the spice blend to your preference for more or less warmth.
- Experiment with different tea varieties for unique flavor profiles.
- Adjust the sweetness and spice level to suit your taste.
- Serve with a slice of lemon for a citrusy twist.

1 cup **20** **10**

Easy

Ethiopian Ginger Tea (Chai Spenja)

Ingredients:

- 1-inch piece of fresh ginger (peeled and sliced)
- 1 black tea bag (Ethiopian or your choice)
- 1 cup boiling water
- Honey or sugar (to taste)
- Lemon juice (optional)
- A sprig of fresh mint (for garnish, optional)

Substitutions

- Adjust the ginger quantity for more or less spice.
- Use your preferred tea variety, such as green tea or herbal tea.
- Customize sweetness to suit your taste, or omit sweeteners for a healthier option.
- Experiment with different citrus fruits for flavor variations.

Chai Spenja, the Ethiopian ginger tea, is a zesty and invigorating beverage known for its soothing properties. It's the perfect remedy for a chilly day or an upset stomach.

Directions

1. In a cup, place the sliced fresh ginger.
2. Add a tea bag to the cup.
3. Pour boiling water over the ginger and tea bag.
4. Let it steep for 5-7 minutes, or until it reaches your desired strength.
5. Remove the tea bag and ginger slices.
6. Sweeten with honey or sugar to taste.
7. Add a splash of lemon juice if desired for extra zing.
8. Garnish with a sprig of fresh mint if available.
9. Sip and enjoy the soothing warmth of Ethiopian Chai Spenja ginger tea.

1 cup   **5**   **10**

Ethiopian Herbal Tea (Koseret Tea)

Koseret tea, an Ethiopian herbal infusion, offers a gentle and calming experience. It's a delicate blend of herbs that refreshes the spirit and soothes the soul.

Ingredients:

- 1 tablespoon dried koseret leaves (Ethiopian basil, or substitute with regular basil)
- 1 cup boiling water
- Honey or sugar (to taste)
- A sprig of fresh basil (for garnish, optional)

Directions

1. Place dried koseret leaves in a cup.
2. Pour boiling water over the leaves.
3. Let it steep for 5-7 minutes to infuse the flavors.
4. Remove the leaves or strain the tea if desired.
5. Sweeten with honey or sugar to taste.
6. Garnish with a sprig of fresh basil if available.
7. Sip and embrace the tranquility of Ethiopian Koseret herbal tea.

Substitutions

- Experiment with other herbal infusions like mint or chamomile for variety.
- Adjust the steeping time to control the flavor intensity.
- Try it iced for a refreshing twist on a hot day.
- Add a slice of orange for a citrusy note.

1 cup   **120**   **10**

Easy

Ethiopian Mango Juice (Mango Sherbet)

Ingredients:

- 2 ripe mangoes (peeled and cubed)
- 1/4 cup sugar (adjust to taste)
- 1 cup water
- Ice cubes (optional)
- A splash of lime juice (optional)

Substitutions

- Adjust the sugar quantity to suit your preference for sweetness.
- Experiment with different mango varieties for varying flavors.
- Add a pinch of chili powder for a spicy kick.
- For a creamier version, blend in a scoop of vanilla ice cream.

Quench your thirst with the tropical delight of Ethiopian Mango Sherbet. It's a sweet and tangy mango juice that's pure sunshine in a glass.

Directions

1. In a blender, combine the ripe mango cubes, sugar, and water.
2. Blend until smooth and the sugar is dissolved.
3. If desired, add ice cubes and a splash of lime juice for extra refreshment.
4. Blend again until the ice is crushed and the mixture is well combined.
5. Pour into a glass and garnish with a mango slice or mint leaves if available.
6. Sip and bask in the tropical goodness of Ethiopian Mango Sherbet!

1 cup   **180 kcal**   **10**

Ethiopian Avocado Smoothie

~~~~~~~~~~~~~~~~~~~~~~~~~~~

Easy

Ingredients:

- 1 ripe avocado (peeled and pitted)
- 1 cup milk (dairy or plant-based)
- 2 tablespoons honey (adjust to taste)
- A pinch of salt
- Ice cubes (optional)
- A squeeze of lemon juice (optional)

Start your day with a creamy and nutritious Ethiopian Avocado Smoothie. It's a blend of avocado, milk, and a hint of sweetness that keeps you energized and satisfied.

Directions

1. In a blender, combine the ripe avocado, milk, honey, and a pinch of salt.
2. Blend until smooth and creamy.
3. If desired, add ice cubes for a chilled smoothie.
4. Add a squeeze of lemon juice for a touch of freshness if you like.
5. Blend again until everything is well combined.
6. Pour into a glass and enjoy your Ethiopian Avocado Smoothie for a nutritious start to your day.

Substitutions

- Customize the sweetness with different sweeteners like agave syrup or maple syrup.
- Experiment with milk alternatives like almond or coconut milk.
- Add a handful of spinach for a green boost.
- Top with chopped nuts for extra crunch.

1 cup **80** **10**

Ethiopian Papaya Juice (Papaya Sharbet)

Easy

Papaya Sharbet is a tropical delight that captures the essence of Ethiopian flavors. It's a refreshing and fruity beverage that's perfect for any time of the day.

Ingredients:

- 1 ripe papaya (peeled, seeded, and cubed)
- 1/4 cup sugar (adjust to taste)
- 1 cup water
- Ice cubes (optional)
- A squeeze of lime juice (optional)
- Fresh mint leaves (for garnish, optional)

Directions

1. In a blender, combine the ripe papaya cubes, sugar, and water.
2. Blend until smooth and the sugar is dissolved.
3. If desired, add ice cubes for a chilled refreshment.
4. Squeeze in lime juice for a zesty twist if you like.
5. Blend again until everything is well combined.
6. Pour into a glass and garnish with fresh mint leaves if available.
7. Sip and savor the tropical goodness of Ethiopian Papaya Sharbet!

Substitutions

- Adjust the sugar quantity to suit your taste preferences.
- Experiment with different citrus juices like orange or lemon.
- Add a pinch of chili powder for a spicy kick.
- For a creamier version, blend in a scoop of vanilla yogurt.

Ethiopian Guava Juice (Guava Sharbet)

~~~~~~~~~~~~~~~~~~~~

Easy

Ingredients:

- 2 ripe guavas (peeled, seeded, and cubed)
- 1/4 cup sugar (adjust to taste)
- 1 cup water
- Ice cubes (optional)
- A squeeze of lime juice (optional)
- A sprig of fresh mint (for garnish, optional)

Guava Sharbet is a sweet and tangy delight that captures the exotic essence of Ethiopian guavas. It's a tropical escape in a glass, perfect for a quick pick-me-up.

Directions

1. In a blender, combine the ripe guava cubes, sugar, and water.
2. Blend until smooth and the sugar is dissolved.
3. If desired, add ice cubes for a chilled refreshment.
4. Squeeze in lime juice for a zesty twist if you like.
5. Blend again until everything is well combined.
6. Pour into a glass and garnish with fresh mint leaves if available.
7. Sip and relish the tropical goodness of Ethiopian Guava Sharbet!

Substitutions

- Adjust the sugar quantity to suit your sweetness preference.
- Experiment with different citrus juices like lemon or orange.
- Add a pinch of ginger for an extra layer of flavor.
- For a creamier version, blend in a scoop of coconut milk.

1 cup | **70** kcal | **15**

Ethiopian Tamarind Drink (Tami)

Easy

Ingredients:

- 2 tablespoons tamarind paste
- 1/4 cup sugar (adjust to taste)
- 1 cup water
- Ice cubes (optional)
- A pinch of salt
- A pinch of ground cumin (optional)
- A squeeze of lime juice (optional)

Tami, the Ethiopian tamarind drink, is a sweet and tangy elixir that awakens the senses. It's a refreshing choice for hot days and a delightful accompaniment to your meals.

Directions

1. In a bowl, combine tamarind paste, sugar, and water.
2. Mix until the tamarind paste is dissolved and the sugar is incorporated.
3. If desired, add ice cubes for a chilled refreshment.
4. Add a pinch of salt and optional ground cumin for depth of flavor.
5. Squeeze in lime juice for an extra zing if you like.
6. Stir well until everything is combined.
7. Pour into a glass and enjoy the vibrant flavors of Ethiopian Tami tamarind drink!

Substitutions

- Adjust the sugar quantity to suit your taste preferences.
- Experiment with different spices like chili powder for a spicy twist.
- Add a splash of soda water for fizziness.
- Garnish with a slice of tamarind for visual appeal.

Chapter 11: Miscellaneous

Ethiopian Berbere Spice Blend

mumummum

Ingredients:

- 1/4 cup paprika
- 2 tablespoons ground cayenne pepper
- 2 tablespoons ground cumin
- 2 tablespoons ground coriander
- 1 tablespoon ground cardamom
- 1 tablespoon ground cinnamon
- 1 tablespoon ground cloves
- 1 tablespoon ground allspice
- 1 tablespoon ground fenugreek
- 1 tablespoon ground ginger
- 1 tablespoon ground nutmeg
- 1 tablespoon salt

Substitutions

- Adjust the spiciness by varying the amount of cayenne pepper.
- Experiment with different ratios of spices to tailor the blend to your taste.
- Use whole spices and grind them for a fresher flavor experience.
- Store in a cool, dry place for long-lasting freshness.

Berbere is the heart and soul of Ethiopian cuisine. It's a complex spice blend with layers of flavor, perfect for adding an authentic Ethiopian touch to your dishes.

Directions

1. In a dry skillet, toast all the ground spices over low heat for about 2-3 minutes, stirring constantly. This releases their aromas and flavors.
2. Remove from heat and let them cool to room temperature.
3. In a bowl, combine the toasted spices with salt.
4. Mix everything well to create your homemade Ethiopian Berbere Spice Blend.
5. Store it in an airtight container away from light and heat.
6. Use this spice blend to add depth and heat to your Ethiopian dishes.

2 tablespoons

200 kcal

30

Normal

Niter Kibbeh (Ethiopian Spiced Butter)

Ingredients:

- 1 cup unsalted butter
- 1/4 cup chopped onions
- 2 cloves garlic (minced)
- 1-inch piece of fresh ginger (minced)
- 1 cinnamon stick
- 2 cloves
- 2 cardamom pods
- 1 teaspoon ground turmeric
- 1 teaspoon ground cumin
- 1 teaspoon ground coriander
- 1/2 teaspoon ground fenugreek
- 1/2 teaspoon ground nutmeg
- 1/4 teaspoon ground cloves
- Salt (to taste)

Substitutions

- Customize the spice blend by adding or omitting spices according to your preference.
- Adjust the salt level to your taste.
- Substitute ghee for butter if you prefer a more pronounced buttery flavor.
- Store in the refrigerator to extend its shelf life.

Niter Kibbeh is the secret ingredient behind many Ethiopian dishes. It's clarified butter infused with aromatic spices, creating a rich and flavorful base for cooking.

Directions

1. In a saucepan over low heat, melt the unsalted butter.
2. Add chopped onions, minced garlic, and minced ginger to the melted butter. Cook gently until the onions become translucent.
3. Add the cinnamon stick, cloves, cardamom pods, and cook for a few minutes until fragrant.
4. Stir in the ground turmeric, cumin, coriander, fenugreek, nutmeg, and ground cloves. Cook for another 2-3 minutes.
5. Remove from heat and let it cool to room temperature.
6. Strain the spiced butter through a fine sieve or cheesecloth to remove solids.
7. Transfer the clarified Niter Kibbeh to a jar, and store it in the refrigerator.
8. Use it as a flavorful base for your Ethiopian dishes or drizzle it on popcorn for a unique treat.

N/A   N/A   10

Mitmita Spice Blend

uuuuuuuuuuuu

Ingredients:

- 2 tablespoons ground cayenne pepper
- 1 tablespoon ground African bird's eye chili (optional, for extra heat)
- 1 tablespoon ground paprika
- 1 teaspoon ground cardamom
- 1 teaspoon ground cloves
- 1 teaspoon ground cumin
- 1 teaspoon ground coriander
- 1 teaspoon salt

Substitutions

- Adjust the spiciness by varying the amount of African bird's eye chili or cayenne pepper.
- Experiment with different ratios of spices to tailor the blend to your taste.
- Be cautious when handling Mitmita, as it's extremely hot. Wash your hands thoroughly after use.
- Store in a cool, dry place for long-lasting freshness.

Mitmita is a fiery Ethiopian spice blend that adds a kick to your dishes. It's not for the faint of heart but perfect for those who crave intense heat and flavor.

Directions

1. In a dry skillet, toast the ground cayenne pepper and optional African bird's eye chili over low heat for about 2-3 minutes, stirring constantly. This intensifies the heat.
2. Remove from heat and let them cool to room temperature.
3. In a bowl, combine the toasted spices with ground paprika, cardamom, cloves, cumin, coriander, and salt.
4. Mix everything well to create your homemade Ethiopian Mitmita Spice Blend.
5. Store it in an airtight container away from light and heat.
6. Use Mitmita sparingly to add fiery flavor to your dishes, and handle it with care.

A small favor to ask

Dear enthusiasts of Ethiopian cuisine and fellow culinary explorers,

As we savor the final morsels of our culinary voyage through the pages of the "Ethiopian Comforts Cookbook: Flavors of Ethiopia - 100+ Authentic Home Comforts Made Easy for Home Cook," I want to extend my deepest gratitude for joining me on this rich and flavorful expedition. Together, we've ventured into the heart and soul of Ethiopian cooking, bringing the authentic and comforting tastes of this diverse cuisine to your very own kitchen.

Now, I come to you with a heartfelt request, one that holds profound significance for us —a small but passionate publishing team. In the realm of cookbooks, reviews are like the essential spices that elevate a dish from good to extraordinary. They are as elusive as the rhythms of Ethiopian music, yet they are the lifeblood of our creative spirit.

If these recipes have allowed you to savor the rich and diverse flavors of Ethiopia, making them accessible and enjoyable for your home cooking, I would be eternally grateful if you could spare a moment. Please return to the app or platform where you acquired this book, and there, you'll find a review button eagerly awaiting your input. A star rating and a brief sentence sharing your thoughts would be the culinary equivalent of a standing ovation in our world.

You see, as a small publisher, every review is a guiding star that illuminates our path. Your words have the power to inspire others to explore the vibrant world of Ethiopian cuisine, creating memorable meals and experiences in their own homes.

Rest assured, every review is not just welcomed but cherished. We understand that, like in any kitchen, even the most skilled chefs may occasionally make a minor mistake. If you happen to spot any such hiccup along the way, please understand that we've poured our hearts into this cookbook. We're human, and in the world of cooking, a touch of imperfection is part of the magic.

From the depths of my heart, thank you for choosing the "Ethiopian Comforts Cookbook," and thank you in advance for considering leaving a review. Your support fuels our passion for creating more delectable, authentic, and accessible culinary experiences. Until we meet again in the pages of another cookbook, may your culinary adventures continue to be filled with the diverse and soulful flavors of Ethiopian cuisine, the joy of home cooking, and the shared delight of meals with loved ones. መልካም የምግብ! (Bon appétit!)

BONUS

In this moment, we're excited to introduce 10 additional bonus recipes from the Garden of Grapes. Be adventurous and try something new that you might enjoy!

Smoked Pork Belly Burnt Ends

Serving Size: 4-6 servings/ Prep Time: 6 hours/ Cal: 450 calories per serving

BONUS

munnununun

Ingredients:

2 lbs pork belly
2 tbsp kosher salt
2 tbsp black pepper
2 tbsp garlic powder
2 tbsp onion powder
2 tbsp paprika
2 tbsp brown sugar
1 cup BBQ sauce

Insider Tips

For extra tenderness, you can wrap the pork belly in foil during the last hour of cooking. Also, make sure to use a meat thermometer to ensure the pork is fully cooked.

Pork belly burnt ends are a delicious and indulgent smoked dish that originated in Kansas City. These bite-sized pieces of tender pork belly are coated in a sweet and sticky sauce, making them a crowd favorite.

Directions

1: In a small bowl, mix together the salt, pepper, garlic powder, onion powder, paprika, and brown sugar.
2: Rub the seasoning mixture all over the pork belly, making sure to cover all sides.
3: Let the pork belly sit at room temperature for 30 minutes.
4: Preheat your smoker to 225°F and add wood chips for flavor.
5: Place the pork belly on the smoker and cook for 4-5 hours, until the internal temperature reaches 190°F.
6: Cut the pork belly into bite-sized pieces and place them in a foil pan.
7: Pour BBQ sauce over the pork belly pieces and toss to coat.
8: Return the pan to the smoker and cook for an additional 1-2 hours.
9: Let the pork belly burnt ends rest for 10 minutes before serving.

4 servings

450 calories

15 minutes

French Dip Sandwiches

Ingredients:

- 2 lbs beef chuck roast
- 1 onion, thinly sliced
- 4 cloves garlic, minced
- 1 cup beef broth
- 1/4 cup soy sauce
- 1 tablespoon Worcestershire sauce
- 1 teaspoon dried thyme
- Salt and pepper to taste
- 4 baguettes, sliced
- Provolone cheese slices for topping (optional)

Substitutions

- Add sautéed mushrooms to the sandwich for an extra layer of flavor.
- Use Swiss cheese instead of provolone for a traditional twist.
- Toast the baguette slices for added crunch.

BONUS

Experience the allure of French cuisine with Slow Cooker French Dip Sandwiches. Succulent roast beef, slow-cooked to perfection, meets crusty baguettes and a savory au jus for a sandwich that is both hearty and satisfying. Let the slow cooker do the work as you savor the classic flavors of a French bistro in the comfort of your home.

Directions

1. Place beef roast, sliced onion, and garlic in the slow cooker.
2. In a bowl, mix beef broth, soy sauce, Worcestershire sauce, thyme, salt, and pepper. Pour over the beef.
3. Cook on low for 6-8 hours until beef is tender.
4. Shred the beef and assemble sandwiches with baguette slices.
5. Optionally, top with provolone cheese and broil until melted.
6. Dip the sandwiches into the savory au jus and relish the French-inspired feast.

Buffalo Chicken Wraps

4 servings   320 calories   20 minutes

Ingredients:

- 1 1/2 lbs boneless, skinless chicken breasts
- 1 cup Buffalo sauce
- 1/2 cup ranch dressing
- 1 cup shredded lettuce
- 1 cup diced tomatoes
- 1/2 cup crumbled blue cheese
- 4 large flour tortillas
- 1/4 cup chopped green onions
- Salt and pepper to taste

Spice up your mealtime routine with Buffalo Chicken Wraps. Inspired by the fiery flavors of Buffalo wings, these wraps are a zesty delight. Slow-cooked chicken bathed in tangy Buffalo sauce, wrapped in a tortilla—it's a culinary escapade that brings the excitement of game day to your table.

Directions

1. Place chicken breasts in the slow cooker and pour Buffalo sauce over them. Cook on low for 4 hours.
2. Shred the chicken and mix with ranch dressing.
3. Assemble wraps with shredded lettuce, diced tomatoes, blue cheese, and Buffalo chicken mixture.
4. Sprinkle with green onions and season with salt and pepper.
5. Wrap and enjoy the spicy goodness.

Tip: Serve with celery sticks for a classic pairing.

Substitutions

- Adjust Buffalo sauce quantity to your spice preference.
- Use blue cheese dressing for added creaminess.
- Wrap in lettuce leaves for a low-carb option.

1 serving   30 minutes

Sesame Crispy Tofu Salad

BONUS

Savor the Sesame Crispy Tofu Salad—a crunchy delight where golden tofu meets the nuttiness of sesame. A dish that's not just a salad but a vegan symphony of flavors!
A vegan symphony of flavors to tantalize your taste buds!

Ingredients:

- 200g firm tofu, cubed
- 2 tbsp sesame seeds
- 2 cups mixed greens
- 1/2 cup shredded carrots
- 1/4 cup edamame
- 2 tbsp sesame ginger dressing
- 1 tbsp soy sauce
- 1 tbsp rice vinegar
- Salt and pepper to taste

Directions

1. Press tofu to remove excess water, then coat with sesame seeds.
2. In a pan, sauté sesame-coated tofu until golden brown.
3. In a bowl, toss mixed greens, shredded carrots, and edamame.
4. In a small bowl, whisk together sesame ginger dressing, soy sauce, and rice vinegar.
5. Drizzle the dressing over the salad.
6. Top with sesame-crusted tofu.
7. Enjoy the vegan symphony of flavors!

Insider Tips

Add a handful of crispy fried onions for an extra crunch.
Drizzle with sriracha for a spicy kick.

4 servings   **45 minutes**   **14g**

Eggplant Rollatini

Immerse yourself in the elegance of Eggplant Rollatini, where thin slices of eggplant are rolled around a savory ricotta filling.

Ingredients:

- 1 large eggplant, thinly sliced lengthwise
- 1 tablespoon olive oil
- 1 cup ricotta cheese
- 1/2 cup grated Parmesan cheese
- 1 egg, beaten
- 1 teaspoon dried oregano
- 1 teaspoon dried basil
- 2 cups marinara sauce
- 1 cup mozzarella cheese, shredded
- Fresh basil for garnish

Substitutions

- Choose small to medium-sized eggplants for more manageable slices.
- Add ground meat to the marinara sauce for a heartier dish.
- Make it ahead of time and bake just before serving for a stress-free meal.
- Serve with a side of sautéed spinach or a light salad.

Directions

1. Preheat oven to 375°F (190°C).
2. Brush eggplant slices with olive oil and bake for 15-20 minutes until tender.
3. In a bowl, combine ricotta cheese, Parmesan cheese, beaten egg, dried oregano, and dried basil.
4. Spread a spoonful of marinara sauce on each eggplant slice.
5. Place a dollop of the ricotta mixture at one end and roll the eggplant slice.
6. Arrange the rolls in a baking dish.
7. Pour the remaining marinara sauce over the rolls.
8. Top with shredded mozzarella cheese.
9. Bake for 20-25 minutes or until bubbly.
10. Garnish with fresh basil.
11. Enjoy the sophistication of Eggplant Rollatini.

4 servings

25 minutes

Sauage and Cabbage Stir-Fry

Ingredients:

- 1 lb smoked sausage, sliced
- 1 small head cabbage, shredded
- 1 onion, sliced
- 1 bell pepper, sliced
- 2 cloves garlic, minced
- 2 tbsp soy sauce
- 1 tsp ginger, grated
- 2 tbsp olive oil

BONUS

This Sausage and Cabbage Stir-Fry is a quick and satisfying low-carb dish. Savory sausage meets crisp cabbage in a flavorful stir-fry that's perfect for busy evenings.

Directions

1. Heat olive oil in a large skillet.
2. Add sausage and cook until browned.
3. Add onion, bell pepper, and garlic. Sauté until vegetables are tender.
4. Stir in cabbage.
5. Mix soy sauce and ginger, pour over the mixture.
6. Cook until cabbage is wilted.
7. Serve and enjoy the simplicity of a flavorful stir-fry.

Insider Tips

Cooking Hack: Opt for low-sodium soy sauce if you're watching your salt intake.

4 servings

20 minutes

9g

Bell Pepper Nachos

Ingredients:

- 4 large bell peppers, halved and seeded
- 1 lb ground turkey
- 1 packet taco seasoning
- 1 cup shredded cheddar cheese
- 1/2 cup diced tomatoes
- 1/4 cup sliced green onions
- 1/4 cup sliced olives
- Sour cream and guacamole for topping

Insider Tips

Cooking Hack: Customize with your favorite nacho toppings. The bell pepper boats bring a colorful crunch; let them be the vibrant maestros.

BONUS

Experience the joy of Bell Pepper Nachos, where vibrant bell peppers serve as the perfect vessel for your favorite toppings.

Directions

1. Preheat the oven to 375°F (190°C).
2. Brown ground turkey in a pan and season with taco seasoning.
3. Place bell pepper halves on a baking sheet.
4. Spoon the seasoned turkey into each bell pepper half.
5. Top with shredded cheddar cheese.
6. Bake for 15 minutes or until cheese is melted and bubbly.
7. Remove from the oven and sprinkle with diced tomatoes, sliced green onions, and sliced olives.
8. Serve with dollops of sour cream and guacamole.
9. Enjoy the vibrant Bell Pepper Nachos.

1 serving **25 minutes** **10g**

Loaded Cauliflower Bake

Ingredients:

- 2 cups cauliflower florets
- 1/2 cup shredded cheddar cheese
- 3 slices cooked bacon, crumbled
- 2 green onions, chopped

BONUS

Unveil the magic of cauliflower with this Loaded Cauliflower Bake. A low-carb delight with the richness of cheese, bacon, and green onions.

Directions

1. Steam cauliflower until tender.
2. Mix in cheese, bacon, and green onions.
3. Bake until cheese melts and bubbles.
4. Serve hot.

Insider Tips

Cooking Hack: Pre-cook cauliflower for a quicker bake. Experiment with different cheese blends for a flavor twist.

Nutella Stuffed Crepes

Ingredients:

1 cup all-purpose flour
2 eggs
1 1/4 cups milk
2 tbsp melted butter
Pinch of salt
Nutella for filling
Powdered sugar for dusting

Thin crepes filled with rich Nutella spread, a decadent treat for breakfast or dessert.

BONUS

Directions

1. In a blender, combine flour, eggs, milk, melted butter, and salt. Blend until smooth.
2. Heat a non-stick skillet over medium heat and lightly grease with butter.
3. Pour a small amount of batter onto the skillet and swirl to coat the bottom evenly.
4. Cook until the edges start to lift and the bottom is golden brown.
5. Flip the crepe and cook the other side briefly.
6. Remove crepe from the skillet and spread Nutella on one half.
7. Fold the crepe in half, then in quarters.
8. Repeat with the remaining batter and Nutella.
9. Dust crepes with powdered sugar before serving.

Insider Tips

Cooking Hacks: You can add sliced bananas or strawberries along with Nutella for extra flavor. Adjust the sweetness by adding more or less Nutella to each crepe.

1 burrito **25 minutes**

S'mores Breakfast Burrito

Ingredients:

1 large flour tortilla
2 eggs (scrambled)
2 tbsp chocolate chips
2 tbsp mini marshmallows
1 tbsp graham cracker crumbs
1 tbsp butter

A unique twist on the classic s'mores, wrapped in a warm tortilla for a delightful breakfast experience.

Directions

1. In a skillet, melt butter over medium heat.
2. Add scrambled eggs and cook until set.
3. Sprinkle chocolate chips, mini marshmallows, and graham cracker crumbs over the eggs.
4. Cook until marshmallows start to melt.
5. Warm the tortilla in a separate skillet or microwave.
6. Place the egg mixture in the center of the tortilla.
7. Roll the tortilla to form a burrito.
8. Serve warm and enjoy the s'mores goodness!

Insider Tips

Cooking Hacks: You can use a tortilla wrap that's slightly toasted for a crispier texture. Adjust the amount of chocolate chips and marshmallows to suit your taste preferences.

www.ingramcontent.com/pod-product-compliance
Ingram Content Group UK Ltd.
Pitfield, Milton Keynes, MK11 3LW, UK
UKHW050055311025
8675UKWH00081B/629

9 798349 548550